"John Bolin immediately engages you in this creatively written book, provoking you to ask deep questions, to dream, and to take action. If you apply just half of what you read here, you might reach the potential God put in you to make a massive impact while you're here on this planet!"

RON LUCE, PRESIDENT OF TEEN MANIA

"John Bolin is an edgy, relevant example of the inspirational and creative leaders God is using to capture the attention of the desensitized masses!"

LISA BEVERE, CONFERENCE SPEAKER AND
BESTSELLING AUTHOR OF *KISSED THE GIRLS AND MADE THEM CRY*

"A must-read, not only for young men still finding their way, but also for young women and seasoned adults. This book will lift the heart and provide inspiration to all who read it."

DICK SCHULTZ, FORMER EXECUTIVE DIRECTOR
OF THE U.S. OLYMPIC COMMITTEE AND THE NCAA

LIFE
UNLIMITED

JOHN BOLIN

Multnomah® Publishers, Inc. *Sisters, Oregon*

LIFE UNLIMITED
published by Multnomah Publishers, Inc.
© 2003 by John J. Bolin

International Standard Book Number: 1-59052-263-X

Interior typeset by Katherine Lloyd, The DESK, Bend, Oregon

Unless otherwise indicated, Scripture quotations are from:
Holy Bible, New Living Translation © 1996.
Used by permission of Tyndale House Publishers, Inc.
All rights reserved.

Other Scripture quotations:
The Holy Bible, New International Version (NIV)
© 1973, 1984 by International Bible Society,
used by permission of Zondervan Publishing House
New American Standard Bible®(NASB) © 1960, 1977, 1995
by the Lockman Foundation. Used by permission.
The Message by Eugene H. Peterson, Copyright © 1993, 1994,
1995, 1996, 2000, 2001, 2002.
Used by permission of NavPress Publishing Group.
All rights reserved.
The Holy Bible, New King James Version (NKJV)
© 1984 by Thomas Nelson, Inc.

Multnomah is a trademark of Multnomah Publishers, Inc.,
and is registered in the U.S. Patent and Trademark Office.
The colophon is a trademark of Multnomah Publishers, Inc.
Printed in the United States of America

MULTNOMAH PUBLISHERS, INC.
POST OFFICE BOX 1720
SISTERS, OREGON 97759
03 04 05 06 07 08—10 9 8 7 6 5 4 3 2 1 0

—————

Dedicated to both of you:
my mother, Vija, and my darling wife, Sarah.
Your love and support
have made the journey possible.

CONTENTS

FOREWORD

God has a dream for every one of us. He has a vision for you to fulfill. He has a purpose, a reason for which you were born.

For each of us, God reveals this plan by His Spirit and His Word and through special relationships with others who instill in us vision and hope. We need to experience God's dream—to see what He sees, and then live in it and fulfill it.

Some people do this, while others fall short and ruin their lives.

Two decades ago, I was praying and fasting in the forest west of Pikes Peak when I started to see a series of pictures in my heart. I saw stadiums full of men worshiping God. I saw a place where people could go to pray and fast for God's blessing on the city where I live, Colorado Springs. I saw a person using a computer to get vital information on global prayer. I saw God moving parachurch ministries into our city that would reach throughout the world with the gospel. I saw God raising up local young men and women and calling them to go and strengthen the church in the world's darkest areas. And I saw a church in our city that would be a catalyst to fulfill all this.

I was twenty-seven years old at the time. Now I'm forty-seven, and every one of those dreams has come to pass. I'm convinced that what I saw back then were God's dreams, and that He has used a group of faithful people to ensure the fulfillment of these plans.

I recently witnessed the fruit of someone else's dream from two decades ago. I was speaking in Lagos, Nigeria, home to the largest church building in the world. This incredibly beautiful building seats more than fifty thousand people and is situated on a magnificent campus that also includes an expansive university. The church, the university, and the supporting ministries on this campus are the results of a dream that was birthed in the heart of an unknown local pastor twenty years ago. Today this church and university provide great hope not only for Nigeria but also for believers throughout the African continent.

All because of a dream from God—and the willingness to live it out.

"Here comes that dreamer!"—that's what Joseph's brothers said to him in Genesis 37. They meant it as a derogatory remark, but in fact it's the difference between mediocrity in life and fulfillment of God's purpose—a fulfillment Joseph experienced to an incredible degree as he went on to become God's instrument for saving all of Egypt plus his own family (the future nation of Israel).

How about you? Would others call you a dreamer? Have you discovered God's dream for you? If so, what are you doing about it?

All of us must invest time, energy, money—our very lifeblood, it seems—in matters like work, family, hobbies, community activities—even church. Sometimes it can all seem mundane. But if we're careful, if we look closely, we'll see that our activities always offer an opportunity to go somewhere, to do something, to make a difference. Dreams don't have to involve public success; your greatest dream can be fulfilled in ways no one will ever notice but you and the Lord—and that will be more than sufficient.

The question, at bottom, is about how we invest what we have here on earth. Some people's investment demonstrates character, integrity, life, and the fulfillment of God's dream. Others invest their time, talents, and relationships differently, and as life goes on, they've missed their opportunity to realize His dream. This is tragic, because these opportunities don't have to be missed. The chance to live life well, to live beyond the mundane, is always before us—as is made clear in the book you hold in your hands.

My friend John Bolin has learned to treasure his dreams from God, and he has a vision of what life can be if you take seriously God's ideas about your potential. I thank God for the passion He's given John to live with excellence without limits and to encourage others to pursue the best version of their own lives.

John rightly believes that too many people are fenced in by a narrow view of their unique role in making this world a better place. They believe their lives are small, perhaps inconsequential. But that's never what God intends, as John tells us.

Jesus said He came to give us life. And not plain, average, routine life, but life "in all its fullness" (John 10:10). That means out of the park and off the charts in every way. Today, God is calling you to a Life Unlimited.

Read this book and the word *average* will permanently disappear from your outlook. Read it and you can develop the tools to see your dreams fulfilled, to embrace your life and your calling, and to live a Life Unlimited by the shadows of the past, the failures of the present, and the anxiety of the future.

John's wisdom helps us understand the vast potential for living a life that's epic beyond our imagination.

To us is promised *every* good thing—friendships that last a lifetime...total health with energy till your last breath...joy in the everyday moments of life...ideas right from the throne room of heaven...and undying passion for God to drive it all. Now that's living!

The whole road map for such an exciting pilgrimage is here in the pages that follow. I urge you to consider living the unlimited, epic adventure God has planned for you. But be prepared—living a dream is much more strenuous than just dreaming it! You'll need the fullness of God operating for you. That fullness is yours if you seek it: "By his mighty power at work within us, he is able to accomplish infinitely more than we would ever dare to ask or hope" (Ephesians 3:20).

Read John Bolin's *Life Unlimited* and dare to see God's dreams for you come true.

—Ted Haggard

ANYTHING BUT AVERAGE

The safest road to hell," wrote C. S. Lewis, "is the gradual one—the gentle slope, soft underfoot, without sudden turnings, without milestones, without signposts."

The safest road indeed. And I'd say the safest way to hell on earth is the same one—boring, humdrum, and above all, *average*.

That's not what I want. And I'm sure it's not what you'd ever settle for, either.

Two Beaches

This book happened because of the distance I traveled between two beaches.

Nearly a decade ago, on the sand at Fort Myers, Florida, I walked hand in hand with my wife, Sarah. As we walked, I considered my life. At the time, nothing was wrong with it; I had a great job, great friends, and money in the bank. On the outside, everything was "fine." But I sensed there was no real adventure, no mystery, no triumph. In a word, my life was *average*. And I was suddenly horrified.

Something happened to me on that beach. I made a decision to rediscover life and the God who makes life meaningful. I imagined, for a moment, what life *could* be like—full, adventurous, real. And I wanted that.

Maybe I was even experiencing the same desires felt by pioneer explorers and adventurers in the past. They longed for something they'd never seen, and their longing became a journey, a quest, a sort of pilgrimage. I knew that's what it had to become for me as well—a pilgrimage from where I was to where God wanted me to be.

Years later, I walked down another beach near Charleston, South Carolina. Everything had changed. This time, I was facing new challenges, incredible odds, and daunting obstacles. In ten years I'd been through a botched business, a spiritual drought, and a heartbreak with a close friend. Everything had been turned upside down. I felt as though I'd entered a war. And I loved it.

I was fighting all right—but for something bigger than me. It was tougher, but it was real. I felt alive. I was living an extraordinary life, and I was thrilled with it. God had taken me from staleness to vitality.

This book is for anyone who's determined not to live an average life. It's also for all those who, like me, may have found themselves trapped. It's for anyone who feels as though life has become a predictable process, where it's easier to trust in yourself rather than lean fully on God.

Getting the Most from This Book

A few tips that can help you gain the most from these pages:

First, at the end of each chapter you'll notice an overview

of that chapter's big ideas. These are the overarching principles you ought to walk away with. Write them down, commit them to memory, and apply them to your life. Occasionally you'll also find a project designed as a creative, hands-on application of the big ideas. You'll find questions to ponder. Take time to read through them and answer them according to your specific situation and phase of life.

And here's my strongest suggestion: *Life Unlimited* is especially designed to be read with someone else—a friend or guide. The Bible says, "As iron sharpens iron, a friend sharpens a friend" (Proverbs 27:17). Of course, you can read this book on your own and still walk away from it a different person. But you'll gain so much more if you commit to read it with a good friend. A friend will spark questions, ideas, and application that you could never realize on your own.

And the best kind of friend to read this book with is a sage—someone you consider to be a mentor. It might be a teacher or a pastor. Whoever it is, it's someone who adds life experience, trust, and ongoing accountability to your reading experience. Consider also serving as a sage for someone else who's reading this book.

If you're reading with another person, I'd suggest you consider meeting together at least once a week to discuss it. Before you meet, take time to read through the chapter and the tools. Be careful not to use the questions and tools as a cut-and-dried formula. Rather, use them as a launching pad. Use the words on these pages as a nudge for your own heart. Dig deep and discover what God is saying to *you* specifically. Allow room for creativity and individual application, and take time to wrestle for the answers.

Another suggestion: Keep a journal as you read. Remember in *The Matrix* where the hero was offered two small pills, one red and one blue? "Take the red one and you'll forget all of this," he was told, "or take the blue one and you'll learn even more." By keeping a journal, you're taking the blue pill. Write down your thoughts, your dreams, even your frustrations as you read in this book. It will help you begin to form your own answers to the life-large questions this book asks.

One last note before we go on: movies are a tremendous picture of what's happening in our culture. So I refer to a lot of different movies in this book, but I'm by no means endorsing every film I mention. I'm simply using them to make a point or pose a question.

So let's begin. Get ready to be challenged and encouraged to see your life—and to live your life—as you never have before.

part one

THE
SHAPE
OF YOUR
STORY

chapter one

THE EPIC LIFE

Your Inescapable Calling

I think it first struck me a few years ago at a Broncos football game.

I was with eighty thousand fans dressed mostly in orange and blue. I was sitting in section 300, row J, seat 5. It was one of the last games for quarterback John Elway, and everyone knew it. The crowd was electric.

Somewhere in the third quarter, I headed to the Domino's Pizza station to recharge. Waiting in line, I accidentally bumped into a woman wearing a worn-out orange jacket with a faded "7" printed on the back. She quickly spun around, looked at me, and cursed. Then she grabbed her pizza and walked away, muttering something under her breath. *You have a nice day, too,* I thought.

I figured she must have been in her early thirties, though I really couldn't be sure. Her eyes seemed like they'd lived eighty years, and the hair poking out from under her baseball cap looked gray to me.

I made it to the front of the line, but somehow couldn't get the woman's face out of my mind. I suddenly realized I hadn't apologized to her. *I need to find her,* I thought. I quickly paid for the pizza, then turned to join the pulsing crowd, all the while looking for the woman. I didn't see her.

I wondered who she was. Was she at the game with her husband or boyfriend, or was she there alone? And why was she so on edge? Maybe she'd just been fired from her job. Maybe she'd just been diagnosed with cancer. Or maybe it actually hurt when I bumped into her. I don't know. But suddenly I was reminded that I wasn't alone. In a sea of humanity, I'd come face-to-face with another person. It's funny how we live and yet sometimes never even see each other at all.

As I found my seat again, I still saw her face. Then it disappeared and something else happened. It was almost as though the entire football game was being played in slow motion while I scanned the crowd. Faces. Thousands of faces. Some sad, some happy, others angry, others completely indifferent.

Then it hit me. Everyone has a story, an epic waiting to unfold. A beginning. An end. And in between, a story to tell. Full of characters and drama. Of tragedy and triumph.

What are their stories? Do they enjoy life? What are their dreams? Have they forgotten them?

Fabulous stories, millions of them. As I looked around the stadium, I began to hear their stories. And for the first time, I saw them. The man sitting all alone with a bucket of popcorn and a small pocket TV. I watched him for nearly five minutes and he never looked up. I wondered what he'd been doing today before coming to the game. Was he satisfied with it, whatever it was?

Or how about the couple sitting behind me? I knew they were together, but they'd hardly said a word to each other. My heart ached for what seemed to be a romance long since faded.

Then there was the lady next to me. She was another story altogether. You would have thought she invented the game of football. She carefully recounted every play to me as if I hadn't just seen it myself. She, too, was alone. (I thought she'd make a great match for the guy with the TV.)

As I watched these people, I couldn't help asking myself, *What are their stories? Do they enjoy life? What are their dreams? Have they forgotten them? And what about God—do they know Him, or even know about Him?*

All Pulled Together

I recently heard someone say that movie theaters are the pulpits of America today. I think there's more truth in that than we like to admit. In movies we learn how to live and love. We're inspired and moved and frightened. Movies have a way of speaking to us as few other things can. They're like poetry put to motion, or a good book that's come alive in a vivid dream. There's just something you gotta love about a bag of popcorn, an ice-cold Coke, and a good movie.

All kinds of movies. There's the drama, for example, like *Gandhi* or *Out of Africa* or *A Beautiful Mind*. These films show us the range and depth of human emotion. They reach down into our hearts and tug at the parts of us that long to connect with others. We watch them and usually leave half crying, but fully ready to be better people.

And there's the action movie, of course. The summer blockbuster was invented to give the action hero a home. Can you imagine July without James Bond or Jackie Chan or the

Terminator? Today they're faster and wilder than ever. Guns fire, heads roll, and tires spin. The action movie gets our blood pumping and our adrenaline rushing. They make us want to run to the gym and conquer the world. And they give McDonald's something to put in their Happy Meals.

And comedies. The other day, I was watching a scene from *Tommy Boy* and just about cracked a rib. If laughter is the best medicine, then comedy is the drugstore of movies. Sometimes we just need to forget about everything around us as we buckle over in laughter, spilling our popcorn.

Then there's the chick flick. *You've Got Mail* or *Sleepless in Seattle* or *Breakfast at Tiffany's*. Girls love these films, and guys pretend to hate them. Basically they're all the same movie— boy meets girl—with different actors. And we all leave bawling (except the guys, of course).

But movies wouldn't be movies without the mother of them all, the one kind of film that pulls all the genres together—the epic. An epic movie combines the passion of romance, the excitement of action, the joy of comedy, and the depth of drama. Think *Braveheart* or *Gladiator* or *Titanic*. Epics leave us not just moved, but changed. They burn a message into our hearts, a message bigger than themselves. They portray men and women who are passionate about life, who are motivated by something deep and meaningful and real, and who struggle and love and laugh and live with all their being.

What is it about heroes like William Wallace or Maximus Meridius or Joan of Arc or Ben-Hur? For them, the pull of "what could be" called them away from the ordinary. It pulled them away from normal and into a life without bounds or limits.

And that's also you and me.

We were created to live an epic life. Not just a romance

or a drama or a comedy or an action adventure. God hasn't called us to be nice and ordinary and average. We were born to live a life that's full in every way. A life that goes beyond limits and barriers. A life of deep meaning and conviction.

The same voice that calls to the epic hero is calling to you. Your life can be more, stretched beyond your widest horizon.

The Biggest Epic

In essence, our lives are meant to be a picture of the grand epic unfolding all around us, the story of a passionate God rescuing us from the ultimate villain. In that ultimate epic, God gives us a picture of what our own life can be.

Jesus said He came to give us life. And not plain, average, routine life, but life "in all its fullness" (John 10:10). That means out of the park and off the charts in every way. Today, God is calling you to a Life Unlimited.

So what's holding you back? Your past? Your mistakes? Your fear? Yourself?

Life Unlimited is about facing down and breaking the limiting forces in our lives so we can fully live. "Old things have passed away," Paul reminds every believer in Christ; "behold, all things have become new" (2 Corinthians 5:17, NKJV). That's *your* life he's talking about. *Average* is gone; behold, *extraordinary* is here. *Mundane* is history; *meaningful* is the new reality. "Life is either a daring adventure," someone once said, "or nothing."

Strong in the Journey

The sons of Korah once prayed, "Blessed are those whose strength is in you, who have set their hearts on pilgrimage" (Psalm 84:5, NIV). A pilgrimage is simply the journey of a pilgrim. That's every Christian's experience in Christ. Our life on earth is a pilgrim journey. Every one of us takes that trip, but we have choices: how we take it, and what we do along the way.

For those who "set their hearts on pilgrimage" (they really *want* this journey!), for those who find strength for the journey in God and not in themselves, there's fulfillment—these are the people who are truly "blessed," as the psalm says. They're thrilled with what God offers them in life. So they keep on giving their "utmost for His highest," as Oswald Chambers expressed it.

They're ordinary people who've been freed to live extraordinary lives. They possess fire in their hearts and life in their eyes. They know that "all men die, but only a few men ever really live," and they're determined to be among those few who truly live—totally, completely, fully.

So they refuse to live according to limits. They refuse the gentle slope and take on the challenging climb. They live to dare great things in the power of their Lord. They believe the only valid measure of limitation in life is the boundlessness of God: "By his mighty power at work within us, he is able to accomplish infinitely more than we would ever dare to ask or hope" (Ephesians 3:20).

True to Their Inner Call

These epic-living people represent the widest possible diversity—men and women, old and young, rich and poor, famous and obscure. They're scattered across our planet living very different lives in very different cultures. But they all have at least one thing in common: They consistently break the mold, stretch the limits, and follow their hearts. They do what others are too afraid or too embarrassed or too tired to do.

These adventurers take the first wild path branching off from the slow road of conventional wisdom. They believe life is a vast, uncharted wilderness waiting to be explored. That it's something to be experienced, not structured. That it's adventurous, high-risk, and out-of-bounds.

They don't believe that to be successful you've got to keep all the rules or draw inside the lines. They resist instructions, regulations, and safety measures. They don't like being managed or manipulated. They know that what makes sense in the classroom or boardroom may make no sense at all in the real world. They think upside down and inside out.

> They take the first wild path branching off from the slow road of conventional wisdom.

And they absolutely can't stand average anything. They reject preassembled, shrink-wrapped tradition. They ignore the accepted, the usual, the unoriginal. They embrace the uncertain, the unexpected, the unforced.

Living out their epic life, they seldom worry about failure. They don't get confused by confusion or disturbed by disturbances. Above life's commotion, they hear an inner voice calling them away from the safe harbors of average and out into the vast ocean of Life Unlimited.

No Formula for Life Unlimited

But there's no formula for this epic life, no one-size-fits-all, no methodical one-two-three procedure for everyone to follow. That's because God created you absolutely unique. His path for you is unlike anyone else's. That's just the way He is. He's an out-of-the-box kind of God. He loves to do things the way no one else would ever consider. Think about it.

He's the one who used a kid to kill a giant.

He's the one who made a bunch of everyday fishermen His A-Team.

He's the one who preached a sermon through a donkey.

The world says the last man standing wins. God says the one who's a servant will one day become the one who leads.

That's the same surprising, unpredictable God who designed a uniquely personal mission for your life. And He's ready for you to grab hold of it.

By the end of this book, I trust you'll come to believe that the ancient words of prophecy are as true for you as for anyone: "The LORD *called* me before my birth; from within the womb he *called* me by name" (Isaiah 49:1, italics mine). My dream is that through these pages you'll have the confidence to look onward to your calling, and gain a clear picture of what your life really *could* be like.

And—that you'll not only gaze at it, but begin to walk toward it. That you'll discover a path—your own unique path—where you can travel with excitement as you follow God's best plan for you. That you'll learn how to shake off average and put on the skin and bones of a fully engaged life.

Your Takeaway

Plot Points

- Your life is a story, an epic waiting to unfold.
- Your life can be more than average—it can be far more, stretched beyond your widest horizons. You're meant to live a life that's full in every way.
- There's no formula for this epic life. You have a unique path to follow.

Dialogue with a Sage

As mentioned in the introduction, the best way to experience this book is by reading it together with someone else, especially a "sage" in your life—someone you respect and look up to, someone who has lived the kind of life you admire and who you trust to help you along the way in your own life. You can use the following questions to discuss this chapter together with your sage—with both of you answering the questions—or with anyone else you're reading the book together with. Or, on your own, write out your answers to the questions in a journal to record your searching and growth toward Life Unlimited.

- What is your own reaction to the thought of living an average life?
- What does the term "epic life" mean to you personally?
- What kind of story has your life been like so far? More of an action story? A comedy? A romance? A drama? Or a full-fledged epic?
- If it's true that there's no formula for the epic life, and that you must discover your own pathway to it…what do you think you'll have to make sure and do in order to find it?
- In what ways, if any, have you settled for "average" in your life?

From the Script

"God can do anything, you know—far more than you could ever imagine or guess or request in your wildest dreams! He does it not by pushing us around but by working within us, his Spirit deeply and gently within us" (Ephesians 3:20, *The Message*).

SOMETHING GREATER

Your Dreams and Purpose

Every epic story needs a reason.

Indiana Jones treads across a snake-filled underground chamber to approach a stone platform where something awaits....

The gladiator Maximus takes off his masked helmet to boldly approach the Emperor Commodus about settling a score....

With blue-painted face, William Wallace shouts, "Freedom!"—and the word echoes across a battlefield in Scotland....

The lost ark of the covenant. Revenge for a murdered wife and son. A country's liberation.

Every hero and heroine needs something greater than themselves to drive them to become what they would normally never be. Something pushes them to do what they otherwise would never attempt. It's a vision so much bigger than simply making life better for themselves. It's a dream that transcends their worries and overshadows their weaknesses. And when it comes into clear view, an adventure is born.

You and I are no different.

Sheer Grandness

The Lord of the Rings, the epic movie trilogy from director Peter Jackson of New Zealand, has ignited a new generation of J. R. R. Tolkien fans. It's clear already that these films have found a secure place in motion picture history. Why? What is it about *The Lord of the Rings* that captivates us?

The action of course is heart stopping and suspenseful, the acting superb, and the sets, special effects, cinematography, costuming, makeup, and musical score all phenomenal works of art. Jackson's attention to detail in every aspect of the production is brilliant. But I think the key to the trilogy's appeal is its sheer grandness. The story's huge scope is almost too much to take in. It's the story of good versus evil, light versus dark. The epic's faithfulness to that theme makes it timeless. As the credits roll, we leave the theater with our hearts on fire.

Deep down, we all want our lives to count for something. That desire is built into us. I think that's why movies like *The Lord of the Rings* and *Saving Private Ryan* stay with us long after the popcorn is gone. Somehow, each of us loves the idea of living for something bigger than ourselves. Frodo left the comfort of hobbit life in the Shire in order to defeat evil's attempt to destroy Middle Earth. In *Saving Private Ryan,* Captain John Miller gave his life to rescue an obscure private in hopes of easing the pain of a mother who'd already lost three sons to war.

Our purpose is about a lot more than simply making our lives more comfortable or enjoyable. We all know it. The grandness of the epic life can't help but draw us. From out of the very core of our being, every one of us seeks to find whatever it is that makes sense out of life, the grand epic waiting to shape our desires and consume our existence. It's the greater mission that gives meaning to every breath, every step, every laugh, every friend, every day.

The Ultimate Epic

For each of us, that greater mission is to be found in the ultimate epic: good versus evil. Christ versus Satan himself. The kingdom of God versus the kingdom of this world. All our stories and poems and songs are variations of this original. No love is greater. No adventure is more thrilling. No villain is more evil. No king is more noble or dashing. No rescue is more daring or more costly.

It's a timeless epic, centered on a great battle for the hearts and minds and souls of mankind.

President James Garfield once asked, "Is there not a spirit stirring within you that longs to know, to do, and to dare?"

> The Spirit of God is compelling you to take up your part in God's story.

That spirit is the Spirit of God compelling you to take up your part in God's story, for God's purpose on this earth. Fortunately, He tells us quite a lot about that purpose.

It's about humanity's *salvation*—we read that God is "not wanting anyone to perish, but everyone to come to repentance" (2 Peter 3:9, NIV).

It's also about the King's fully recognized *authority*—"And this is his plan: At the right time he will bring everything together under the authority of Christ—everything in heaven and on earth" (Ephesians 1:10).

And it's especially about His own eternal *glory*—"May he be given glory in the church and in Christ Jesus forever and ever through endless ages. Amen" (Ephesians 3:21). "Glory and honor to God forever and ever" (1 Timothy 1:17).

And we know that all this will absolutely be accomplished, because "the LORD's plans stand firm forever; his intentions can never be shaken" (Psalm 33:11). That's what the winning side is all about.

Our involvement with God's epic story is the ultimate

reason for life itself. And it fuels the best and highest dreams that God inspires within us.

Dream Explosion

Dreams. They're born on mountaintops, on altars, and in notes jotted on napkins. Usually, they come alive so quickly that we wonder if they've really been born at all. Often they begin as just a passing thought. Then they grow, nagging at our thoughts and slowly stealing away our passion. When we finally give in totally to them, they explode inside us.

As a youth pastor, I watched it happen over and over again. Young people seeing for the first time what God had been seeing for them for millions of millennia. Building orphanages, pastoring a church, pioneering a business, creating a masterpiece. Taking their place in God's great epic by working with their hands or their heads or their hearts.

It's discovering what I call your "magnificent obsession." It's the thing that's most *you,* and that you long to do as your contribution to the eternal epic.

So I dare you: Dream the biggest dreams for God you've ever dreamed.

My good friend Rachel Blaha likes to talk about what she calls the "extreme dream." The other day, she asked me, "John, what would you do for God if you knew you couldn't fail?" Rachel herself just turned twenty-one and has a dream to impact Hollywood for God. And you know what? She'll do it. Just this morning I heard that she's landed her first commercial role. She's not afraid to allow the plans of God to burn through her and touch the world.

So, what's your own extreme dream?

Whatever it is, don't squelch it. What if Joseph in the Old Testament had questioned the dreams God gave him, and written them off as his own imagination or selfish ambition? What if Noah had done the same with the words he heard from God about building an ark? Or what if Paul responded with the same disregard for his vision on the road to Damascus, and for the Lord's promise that Paul would become His witness to the nations?

Beyond Your Flaws

I love what King Arthur tells Lancelot in the movie *First Knight*. The young Lancelot, who seemed to appear out of nowhere, has just surprised everyone with his bravery, daring, and swordsmanship. Arthur sees in him incredible potential, and tells him, "You care nothing for yourself…just the passionate spirit that drives you on. God uses people like you, Lancelot, because your heart is open. You hold nothing back, give all of yourself."

Lancelot shrugs off the compliment. "If you knew me, you wouldn't say such things."

Arthur quickly responds: "I take the good with the bad. I can't love people in slices."

Like God, Arthur understood the gap between Lancelot's true self and the false one he'd begun to believe in. He was able to look past his flaws and saw instead an epic life in the making.

He also saw a man who was living without a cause. Earlier in the film, Arthur tells Lancelot, "If you must die, die serving something greater than yourself. Better still—live and serve." For Arthur and, later, Sir Lancelot, Camelot was that "something greater" to live for. It represented brotherhood and peace and true love. In many ways, Camelot is like a picture of the kingdom of God—the heart of the epic life.

All the talent, good looks, personality, and brains in the

world are meaningless unless we have a greater "why" to spend them on, and a motivation that transcends them. Arthur understood that well. He knew that if you give a man a purpose, he'll come alive. He knew that a greater good is the key ingredient for an unlimited life.

Camelot at Summer Camp

I remember the first time I caught a glimpse of the Something Greater. It came at the climax of my junior high years, which was not exactly a trouble-free time period for me.

I have distinct memories from those days of my mother crying her eyes out and praying for every one of us six kids, especially me. My dad had prayed with me when I was younger and gave my life to Christ, and he continued to lead our family in devotions every night. We read through the Bible a number of times during my junior high and high school years. And besides being a spiritual example, Dad was my best friend. He took me camping and fishing, patiently walked me through my first romance, and was later the best man in my wedding.

I was doing lots of things wrong.

Mom and Dad were careful about what we watched on TV and who we chose as friends, and only rarely did we miss church. But while my parents were doing so many things right, I was doing lots of things wrong.

I think it started when I made a friend against my mother's intuition. David was a rebel. His father had abandoned his mother, and the hole in David's heart left him frustrated and angry. Unsure of how to handle it, he went wild and brought me along for the ride. I was only fourteen, but that year I tasted my first tobacco, drank my first beer, and discovered for the first time what a naked woman looked like (in pictures, anyway). One day, David brought something to school he called a Chinese throwing star. He showed me how to throw the small piece of metal against a wall and make it stick. I though it was the coolest thing I'd ever seen. A few days later, Mr. Ward walked in just as I chucked one of them into the bathroom wall. He didn't think it was quite as cool as I did. My tenure as a junior high student ended that day—I was expelled.

Sitting on the bench in front of school at the end of the day, I still remember the sinking feeling in my stomach as my dad pulled up in our blue and white Ford van with my brother and sisters. *I'm so busted,* I thought as I slumped into the backseat. I knew that he knew, and that my brother and sisters did also. But no one said a word all the way home.

That night, I sat with my parents and we talked and cried until nearly midnight. Though they were forgiving and understanding, I could see the deep disappointment in their eyes. It's the worst sight in the world for a kid. My innocence and conscience had been bruised. I felt like a failure. I knew I'd embarrassed my parents and I felt totally defeated and personally deflated. I wanted to run away. It was the lowest point in my fourteen short years.

That summer I would gaze upon Camelot for the first time in my life. I would feel the hot steel of the sword of God on my shoulder, and everything would change.

My parents made me attend a summer youth camp in Lexington, Nebraska. Reluctantly, I agreed (as if I had any choice in the matter). Even at the camp, my past decisions seemed to stick with me. I felt so guilty for the things I'd done that year in school that I refused to attend the nightly meetings. My friends and I sneaked into our cabin, covered the window, and carefully put towels under the door so no light shone through. We spent our time listening to music and lighting aerosol deodorant on fire.

One night, for some reason, I decided to go to the meeting. I sat in the back of the room and figured that I blended well with the hundreds of other kids there. Somehow, God picked me out of the crowd. I can't tell you exactly what happened that night, but I can tell you that God got ahold of me. And my life—from His perspective—suddenly made sense. It was my first taste of something bigger than myself as a life purpose. I sensed God challenging me, as Arthur did with Sir Lancelot, to live a life of meaning and destiny.

The Compass Inside You

You were created with a compass inside you pointing in the direction of God's design, God's mission. You weren't created to fit into any mold other than the one God specifically created for you. And you'll never be truly satisfied until you find it.

You were born *on* purpose, and *with* a purpose—created *by* God, *for* God. The Bible tells us, "We are God's workmanship, created in Christ Jesus to do good works, which God prepared in advance for us to do" (Ephesians 2:10).

David once said confidently, "The LORD will fulfill his purpose for me" (Psalm 138:8, NIV). You can say that, too, with just as much confidence. And know for certain that this purpose isn't ultimately for your sake, but for His. In fact, Scripture actually says, "Obsession with self in these matters is a dead end; attention to God leads us out into the open, into a spacious, free life" (Romans 8:6, *The Message*).

At the end of the day, striving only to make life better for ourselves will end in certain frustration. But focusing our time and energy on His kingdom, His Camelot, will lead us to "a spacious, free life." That's what we're looking for—a life that's full and meaningful and free.

Plot Points

- In the core of your being, you're seeking a greater mission, the most significant purpose for your life. You were created for something far bigger than yourself.
- Your involvement with God's epic story is the ultimate reason for your existence. You were created *by* God, *for* God.
- God created you with a compass inside you pointing in the direction of His design for you. In line with that design, He will instill within you dreams and a vision for your future.

Dialogue with a Sage

- What is your own "extreme dream"? What other dreams, if any, do you believe God has given you?
- How would you define your mission and purpose in life as you understand it now?
- How would you characterize what your understanding is of God's design for you? What shape and form has He given you in terms of your longings, interests, abilities, and thought patterns?

From the Script

"God speaks again and again, though people do not recognize it. He speaks in dreams" (Job 33:14–15).

chapter three

LIFE LIST

Your Goals and Plans

I have a tradition every year—right around January—of taking a few days and getting away from slamming doors and beeping phones, and retreating into the mountains. Usually I'll toss my fly rod and a few good books into the car, then drive until I feel like stopping. It's my way of refocusing my head and recalibrating my heart.

A few years ago on one of these trips, I took along a copy of *Chicken Soup for the Soul*. On day two of my retreat, having settled into a cabin nestled in the Colorado Rockies, I sat down with the book.

From Dreams to Goals

One of the stories inside that especially caught my attention was about a man named John Goddard, a highly honored explorer whose life is captured well by the motto "To dare is to do, to fear is to fail." Decades ago, at age fifteen, Goddard sat down and gave written form to his teenage dreams by compiling a list of 127 goals for the rest of his life.

Given his youthful explorer's bent, it isn't surprising that the vast majority of those goals had to do with exploring and experiencing different places all around the globe—climbing the Matterhorn and Mount Fuji, exploring the Amazon and the Nile, visiting the Great Wall of China and the Taj Mahal and the Eiffel Tower and the Pyramids, retracing the travels of Marco Polo and Alexander the Great across Asia, photographing Niagara Falls, studying primitive cultures in the Congo and Alaska and Brazil, following the River Jordan from the Sea of Galilee to the Dead Sea, swimming in Lake Superior, exploring the depths of the Red Sea, and traveling down the Grand Canyon by foot and by boat. There were scores of entries like those.

Also on his list were dozens of encounters in more obscure locations—exploring the Rio Coco in Nicaragua, climbing Ayers Rock in Australia and Mount Huascaran in Peru, visiting the Sacred Well of Chichen-Itza in Mexico, observing dragon lizards on Komodo Island, watching a cremation ceremony in Bali, and so on.

Lots of other items Goddard listed had to do with acquiring knowledge and skills—such as learning to play the flute and violin and piano, learning jujitsu and polo and fencing, flying a plane, building a telescope, writing a book, composing music, running a five-minute mile, lighting a match with a .22 rifle, learning Spanish and French and Arabic, reading all the Bible plus significant works of eighteen of the world's most famous writers, becoming familiar with music by fifteen of the world's most famous composers, and teaching a college course.

Also on the list were plenty of fun experiences like riding a horse in the Rose parade, diving in a submarine, flying in a balloon, shipping aboard a freighter as a seaman, and visiting a movie studio.

Next to last on his list—goal number 126—was "Marry and have children" (understandably low in priority, I suppose, for a boy of fifteen). And last but not least, number 127 was "Live to see the twenty-first century."

Here's what's amazing: By the time Goddard was in his seventies, he'd accomplished well over 100 of those 127 goals, including every single one that I've mentioned above.

As I sat on the bed in that cabin, with my dog Indiana snoozing at my feet, and read over Goddard's list, I thought about my own life and asked myself, "Why not?" I pulled out a pad of paper and a pen and started writing.

I'd written things I'd never tell anyone else.

Something happened I never expected: I *kept* writing. And writing. One hundred and fifteen goals later, I stopped. At nearly 1:00 A.M., I put down my pen and read through the words on the page, and I couldn't help but smile. I'd written things I'd never tell anyone else.

I shut off the light, and as I lay there in the cabin's darkness, I wondered what it would be like to actually accomplish all the things I'd written down.

Then it hit me. *What am I doing?* I'd come to the mountains for a retreat with God, to get my heart reconnected with His. Suddenly I was aware that I'd spent the past hour or more totally consumed with myself. Or so it seemed.

Tomorrow, I'll focus on God, I told myself, as I drifted off to sleep.

My retreat passed, and I kept the list stored neatly on one of the dozens of legal pads that were home to my writing and research. And there it stayed.

What was the right thing to do with those goals? Ignore them, as mere selfish yearnings? Or embrace them as something from God, and make the most of fulfilling each one?

Plans from God

Jesus once called the devil the father of lies. I wonder if perhaps one of his greatest lies is to have us believe that any desire burning in our hearts is necessarily selfish and ungodly. That to have dreams or goals or ambitions is somehow evil or less than holy.

I believe the enemy would love nothing more than to convince you to be satisfied with life as it is. Do nothing. Be nothing. In essence, waste your life and bottle up your worship. He'll always be trying to derail our dreams and goals.

Am I saying I think we're free to do whatever we want and to follow whatever selfish pursuit pops into our head? Of course not. God never says we can do whatever we want, and He gives us no permission to be the author of our own lives. But He does have big plans for you and me, plans that He faithfully plants in our hearts, in our minds, and in our dreams. And there's nothing wrong with that. In fact, that's one of the most helpful ways He works in our lives.

God gave Moses specific plans for building the Tabernacle. He gave Joseph economic plans to rescue Egypt. And He gave His prophets all kinds of specific plans for what to do and what to say to God's people. There's nothing wrong with making plans. On the contrary, God tells us, "The noble man devises noble plans; and by noble plans he stands" (Isaiah 32:8, NASB). That must mean there's such a thing as plans that *aren't* noble. What's the difference? The difference is the motivation in our hearts. If your heart is right with God, He's got destiny waiting for you, and He'll make sure to give you good plans for living it out.

And it's only these that allow us to escape our selfishness.

In *The Lord of the Rings: The Fellowship of the Ring,* Frodo's quest to destroy the Ring of Power wasn't driven by selfish ambition. His goal was to rescue Middle Earth from a catastrophic danger which very few people fully understood. The plan for accomplishing this goal, though fairly simple, was incredibly daring and required the utmost from Frodo in patience, endurance, and sacrifice. By doing the right thing— the unselfish thing—at this most crucial moment in Middle Earth's history, Frodo achieved incomparable fulfillment and lasting glory as a hero.

That's the success paradox. Accomplishing great things— plus establishing the right plans 'and goals to pull them off—is far from selfish, even though it brings us the greatest personal benefits imaginable.

In the way all this works, everything about it is a paradox. To succeed, we have to surrender. When we turn from self and put our faith in Christ, God's heart is transplanted within us with power to overrule our selfish hearts. His very life becomes ours. Out of His life and heart beating within us, His visions become ours, His ideas become ours, His plans become ours—visions and ideas and plans straight from the throne room in heaven. Suddenly we're plugged into timeless significance, because "the LORD's plans stand firm forever" (Psalm 33:11).

David understood this. That's why he shares with God's people this prayer: "May he grant your heart's desire and fulfill all your plans" (Psalm 20:4). And it's why Solomon counsels us, "Commit to the LORD whatever you do, and your plans will succeed" (Proverbs 16:3, NIV). That doesn't mean we can commit to God our plans for robbing a bank and expect to get away clean with the money. The motivation behind our plans must be God-focused. To commit anything to the Lord, we have to first be fully committed to Him ourselves.

"Delight yourself in the LORD and he will give you the desires of your heart" (Psalm 37:4, NIV). This verse has been used and abused by many who fail to recognize how God is giving us an if/then statement: Delight yourself in God—love Him, embrace Him, worship Him; *if* you do that, *then* He'll give you your heart's desires. The verse isn't saying you can have whatever you want; it's saying God will ensure that your desires are His. He'll infuse you with His passions. If you're delighting yourself in Him, your desires and your goals will be more naturally His desires, His goals.

And God Himself will make the achievement of those goals possible by an amazing flow of energy that He carries on right inside us: "By his mighty power at work within us, he is able to accomplish infinitely more than we would ever dare to ask or hope" (Ephesians 3:20).

Nothing Little

The distinguished Chicago architect and city planner David Burnham once wrote, "Make no little plans. They have no magic to stir men's blood and probably themselves will not be realized. Make big plans; aim high in hope and work." I believe God engraves those same words on your heart: *No little plans.*

> God engraves the words on your heart: *No little plans.*

When we pull back and refuse to be all God created us to be, when we have only little plans, we're shorting God. We're supposed to be His hands extended to our world, and that's why we're accountable for how we manage His gifts and talents.

Over time I came to realize that the "life list" I drew up

that night in my mountain cabin was really God's desires rushing out of my heart and onto paper. When I wrote the list, I was passionate for God and hungry for His Word. I was simply His child, receiving good things flowing down to me through our heavenly Father's grace. I think that's why they so easily fell from my pen to the page.

Since then, I've gone back to my list and refined and rewritten it. I've surrendered it to God and repented for not pursuing it. And I've begun checking off different goals as I accomplish them. In the past four years, nearly a third of them have been achieved, to the glory of God.

Putting Your Dreams to Work

Generally, our dreams and goals and plans will come together at the intersection of our gifts and talents and work. The Bible says, "God has given each of us the ability to do certain things well" (Romans 12:6). Every one of us has ability and talent that we can use as part of our role in the Great Epic.

Paul emphasized that we're to actually *use* these gifts and abilities God has given us for the benefit of others (Romans 12:6–8). Peter did the same: "Each one should use whatever gift he has received to serve others" (1 Peter 4:10, NIV). Some people say, "I don't know what to do," or "I don't really have any great vision or special talent to give to it." Moses said pretty much the same thing when God spoke to him at the burning bush: "I'm a nobody. Besides, what if no one listens?"

How did God answer? "Moses, what is in your hand?" For Moses, it was a staff. Think about that for a minute. It wasn't a crown or a scepter or a sword. It was a simple stick. And it became one of the greatest supernatural weapons in all of human history.

So what's in *your* hand? What do you already have in

your possession? Speaking ability? Artistic ability? Money? Friendships? All of us have something we can use to accomplish our part in God's work here on earth, as we serve one another.

Few people spend their lifetime doing what they love, but *you can be one of them.* In God's coming kingdom, we'll all have the thrill of reigning with God by using our divine combination of talent and labor, with restored bodies and minds. In the meantime we have the opportunity to practice the same thing as we tune up our vehicles and speed at full throttle toward that magnificent obsession. After all, if this life really is the dress rehearsal for the rest of eternity, let's be totally prepared for opening night!

Examining Who You Are

God created you with your distinct likes and dislikes for a reason. He had a reason for making you artistic or mathematical or analytical. The Bible says, "There are different ways God works in our lives, but it is the same God who does the work through all of us" (1 Corinthians 12:6).

God has created you with gifts and talents that, if used, will advance this overall mission for the kingdom of God. It's up to you to use them, as God unfolds the details about how you can most effectively carry out His plan and vision for you. It means saying, "I can fulfill my part of God's plan by _____" (and you complete the sentence). Or "I'm best suited to preach the gospel when I'm _____" (and you complete the sentence). That's your dream, your vision.

If John Goddard can accomplish so much during his lifetime, what can you do? What are the divine goals and plans that lie deep inside you? What are the secret ambitions God has planted in your heart that are waiting to come alive? You may not come up with 127 items, but that's fine. Maybe it's just a handful of targets, but you're absolutely convinced they're from God.

Or you might find yourself saying, "I could never accomplish everything I have in my heart to do. I'm not qualified enough. I'm not smart enough. I'm not strong enough." Imagine if Frodo had said that and given up his quest! Even worse, what if Paul or Peter or Esther or Daniel had reacted that way?

God loves to take the humble, unsuspecting hero and use him to turn the world upside down. Two thousand years ago, He did it with twelve ordinary men who were only fishermen and tax collectors and such.

And now He's ready to do it with you.

Your Takeaway

Take some time to make your own "life list." Simply write what naturally comes from your heart. Do it as an expression of your worship for God and your gratefulness for how He has made you. And don't worry about whether any of your goals are totally your own ideas rather than seeds planted by God. "You can make many plans, but the LORD's purpose will prevail" (Proverbs 19:21). He'll accomplish whatever plans of these He wants for you, as you remain flexible and humble.

Plot Points

- God has big plans for you that He faithfully plants in your heart, in your mind, and in your dreams.
- Our enemy, the devil, will always be trying to derail these plans and goals. One of his greatest lies is that

anything that's burning in your heart to do is merely selfish.

- To succeed in accomplishing what God wants you to, you have to surrender to Him.

Dialogue with a Sage

- How have your dreams, goals, and plans for your life changed over time? To what do you attribute these changes?
- How would you define the word *goal* and *plan?*
- What does it really mean to surrender to God?
- What activities in life make you feel most alive?
- After making your life-list, look over these goals you've written down. Which would you say are most urgent or important? Which are you most passionate about? What deadlines, if any, should you attach to some of them?

From the Script

God's words to His people: "I know what I'm doing. I have it all planned out—plans to take care of you, not abandon you, plans to give you the future you hope for" (Jeremiah 29:11, *The Message*).

chapter four

BEYOND THE DOOR

Finding Freedom

Remember the scene with me...

The waves suddenly stop, almost as if turned off by some giant mechanism deep beneath the ocean. Alone in his small boat, the man finds his terror dissolving into relief. The angry clouds practically disappear, and sun rays glisten against the calming water.

Totally exhausted, Truman slumps in the boat and looks upward. For the first time in his life he sees it: The blue sky suddenly appears like a colossal cyclorama arching over and around him. He's only a few feet from the "horizon" he'd always thought was endless sky. And in those shades of blue he makes out the shape of a door.

He's totally confused. This is a real ocean that's supposed to lead to Europe or Africa or some other exotic place. What's happening?

The Human Show

His boat bumps against the backdrop. Still dazed, wondering if he's dreaming, he reaches out for the recessed door handle.

"Truman!" The voice booms out of nowhere.

At first, Truman is sure it's God. But it's actually a TV producer who begins explaining that Truman is the star of *The Truman Show,* a popular program that's been running since he was born. Truman's life has been confined to a massive movie set, and his family and friends and everyone he's encountered in his hometown of Seahaven have all been actors. Every moment, every move of his existence has been captured on camera for the world to watch—which they have been doing, in every corner of the globe, for thirty years.

"You're the star," the producer says, "of a show that gives hope and joy and inspiration to millions."

Truman shakes his head, slowly taking in this haunting reality of his so-called life. His eyes well with tears. He's half afraid, half furious. "Nothing was real?" he shouts.

"*You* were real," the booming voice replies. "And that's what made you so good to watch. Truman, there's no more truth out there than in the world I created for you—the same lies and deceit. But in my world, you have nothing to fear."

Silence. Then Truman turns, and viewers around the world inhale with a collective gasp as he pushes open the door to reveal the backside of a giant set. A few steps, and he's out of sight. The television screens go blank. *The Truman Show* is over. But Truman's life has finally begun. For the first time he feels alive. For the first time in his life he's free.

The unsuspecting and dramatically average Truman had lived what he thought was a typical life. He had a job, a home, a best friend. Everything, it would seem, was perfect— or at least, perfect enough. After all, that was the way the show was created to be.

And so it had gone day after day, year after year. Until one day Truman had done something the creators of the show never expected. He began to wonder. He began to wonder if there was more to life than what he knew. He began imagining what the world was like outside of Seahaven. The producers tried, without success, to distract Truman and settle him down. It didn't work. He wanted to see the world. And he wanted someone to see it with.

He fell in love with Susan, one of the actresses placed on the show as an extra. The romance was unscripted, so the producers pulled her from the show. When Susan didn't show up the next day, Truman wondered where she'd gone. Hungry for love and life, he set out to see the world and find Susan. But there was a problem: The only way out of Seahaven was across the ocean, and Truman was scared to death of the water.

He faced his greatest fear.

So he did something the producers never expected. He faced his greatest fear.

When he did, everything changed. And he went on to discover true freedom.

Unlimited

I believe that discovering your mission and goal for the epic life will bring a dynamic encounter with personal freedom beyond anything you've ever known.

None of us were born to live in a cage. We aren't made to be boxed in or preprogrammed. As Truman discovered, there's more to life than meets the eye. And like Neo found out in *The Matrix,* we have a choice either to stay in the assumed comfort and safety of our world or to explore something riskier but better.

For us, that something else is what *can be* in the life God planned for us. A life beyond the facade. One not bound by someone else's expectations or plans. Free from false realities or self-imposed limitations. A life that in every way is truly...*unlimited*.

The Oxygen of the Soul

Israeli military hero Moshe Dayan called it "the oxygen of the soul." There's nothing in the world like freedom.

Ask the guy who walks out the front gate of a prison and onto the street for the first time in twenty years. Ask the woman who pays off her final credit card bill after living for months or years under the burden of debt. Or consider an animal released back into the wild after living in captivity.

The other day I watched a *National Geographic* special on TV. Two orcas—killer whales—were being released into the ocean after years of living in a huge aquarium at a theme park. The documentary showed pictures of the two whales jumping out of the water at the water park, snatching pieces of fish from the hands of the trainers and performing with twists and flips on command.

The two whales seemed sadly trapped in their glass tanks. That, of course, isn't where killer whales are supposed to live.

If you've ever watched killer whales in the wild, you know there are few things more awesome. I remember my first encounter with them. A few years ago, I was on a small boat one morning in the waters just off Ketchikan, Alaska. We were steelhead fishing and came upon a good school of salmon. We lowered our bait and waited for our rods to lunge. But the salmon never took our bait, and we wondered why.

A moment later, we knew. Three giant killer whales launched out of the water no more than fifty feet from the bow of our small boat. The water churned with the force of their massive bodies. Their razor sharp teeth glistened in the brilliance of the sun. I can't express the wildness of that moment. I saw in these fish what Jack London saw in wolves of the North. I felt suddenly very small.

These creatures weren't made to be locked in or hand-fed or whistled at. They were born to roam freely and eat what they want, when they want.

Watching the whales on the *National Geographic* show, I felt sorry for them. They'd missed more than half their life. It was almost as if they'd never been born. *But,* I thought, *it's never too late.*

As those two giant creatures swam away from the shore and into the deep for the first time in their lives, I could only imagine how they felt. For the first time they realized that water doesn't have to end. For the first time they could move as they were made to move. They could jump when they felt it, not when a whistle blew. They could roam and hunt rather than wait to win food.

They weren't made to be locked up. And you and I weren't, either. "Christ has really set us free," Paul says. "You have been called to live in freedom" (Galatians 5:1,13). Freedom is your calling, your privilege, your gift, your destiny.

The Tragedy of Limits

So how does it happen that we lose our freedom?

Somewhere between ages twelve and thirty, a lot of us seem to accept that our lives are limited. I don't remember exactly when that happened to me. But at age twenty-eight (on that Florida beach walk that I mentioned), I was shocked to realize I'd become a victim to it. I'd begun to believe an average life was okay. For a lot of us, we get used to whatever's around us and accept the lie that certain limits will always be there to keep us in. We believe there may not be any reality beyond this movie set, or any ocean outside this tank.

And when we think that way, I can imagine God looking down at us and asking, "Who told you that you have those limits?" He hates the idea of walls and bars and seawalls that rob us of life. "You will go free," He promises, "leaping with joy like calves let out to pasture" (Malachi 4:2). And Jesus says that whoever He sets free is "free indeed!" (John 8:36, NKJV). No ifs, ands, or buts. The very reason He stretched out His arms and bled and died on that hill was so we could break free of average and live. Really live.

> I'd begun to believe an average life was okay.

That's why He's grieved whenever we limit our lives and fail to accept His gift of freedom. What could be more tragic? "Many people die with their music still in them," Oliver Wendell Holmes observed. "Why is this so? Too often it's because they are always getting ready to live. Before they know it, time runs out." Are you still "getting ready to live," or are you really living? You can't afford to die with your music still in you. You've got to take the leap, open the door, and jump out.

Take the Freedom Road

Count on it: The epic life is a life of freedom. Freedom to step away from average. Freedom to open the door of your current "reality." And freedom to be the person God created you to be.

Finding that freedom may not be easy. It might mean digging deep and uncovering a hidden wound that has kept you boxed in. It might mean that you, like Truman, will have to face your greatest fear.

But once you've done that—once you've begun to recognize your life's mission and to experience the wind-in-your-face freedom of pursuing it—you'll also start to discover yet another exciting dynamic of Life Unlimited. We'll take a closer look next at what Jesus really has in mind when He promises us life "in all its fullness."

Your Takeaway

Plot Points

- God wants you to be free so you can fully serve Him.
- Your current view of "reality" may not be God's true reality.
- Facing your fears can open the doors to freedom.
- God is grieved when you limit your life and fail to accept His gift of freedom.

Dialogue with a Sage

- In what ways, if any, do you feel trapped? What would it take to get free?
- What do you think it really means for you to be free, from God's perspective?
- Is freedom the same thing as having permission to do anything you want? If not, what's the difference?
- What in your life represents the doorway to freedom?

From the Script

"God purchased you at a high price. Don't be enslaved by the world" (1 Corinthians 7:23).

chapter five

FULL THROTTLE

Fully Engaged Living

We watch them in action, and we love it.

Under incredible pressure, facing impossible odds, they sense every lurking danger and prepare to overcome it. They know how to fight with weapons or their bare hands or any object lying nearby. With strategic shifts and spins, with fearless leaps and plunges, with perfectly aimed strikes and blows they thwart an enemy's onslaught and rescue themselves and their defenseless friends or even the entire world from evil's grip.

And all the while they're brutally in touch with their inner self—they're poetic, romantic, spiritual, and incredibly swift and strong, all at the same time.

Everyone's got their favorite action heroes. And the thing that sets them apart is their full-on lifestyle. They live in overdrive. Every cylinder seems to be striking at the speed of light and in perfect harmony. They move forward with boundless energy, intense spirituality, shining personality, and contagious personal passion. They're out of the box and out of the ordinary.

We've all sat with a tub of popcorn and admired these guys. Oh, to be one of them! But then, they're only figments of Hollywood's imagination, right?

Maybe not.

Full Engagement

I remember as a kid putting a sheet over my shoulders, putting on my construction-paper mask, and donning my "secret weapons." Decades later, my two sons are constantly jumping off furniture and spinning in circles and hitting each other with the same secret weapons. Something in all of us loves the thought of pretending to be the action hero.

But what if you really *could* be one of them? What if I told you your life could make James Bond jealous? Can you imagine living with more passion than angel/agent Natalie Cook? You can. In fact, that's exactly what God intends for your life.

I call it *fully engaged living,* and it's the secret weapon you'll need to ultimately accomplish your God-given mission and make the most of your God-given freedom. I'm not talking about caffeine-induced, high-strung, nonstop motion and activity. That's a recipe for burnout. I'm talking about living to the extreme in every aspect of your life—as marked out by a trustworthy matrix we'll look at in just a moment.

We all know full-throttle people. We love to be around them. When they're in the room, things just happen. They're magnets of energy and passion. They've come to grips with God's design for them and have determined to live intensely in every way. They don't allow adversity or tough times to determine their attitude or their future. They live to serve others and love God. They manage their energy and are conscious of their health. And they live with a clear and present strategy for accomplishing God's purpose. They may not be superheroes, but they're supersurrendered to God's plan.

They include both women and men. Some are wealthy and some are just getting by. They're extroverts and introverts. They're people in the ministry and in the marketplace. And the one thing they all have in common is that they've learned how to live it up.

Like you, I know many of them who've inspired my life—Cliff, Susan, Christopher, Robert, Brigit, Barry, Ted, Doug, Michael, Tammy, Brandon, Terry, Layne, Ken, Charlie, Thomas, and Nikki, to name a few. I've watched their lives and I can tell you, fully engaged living is possible. And all these friends learned it ultimately from the all-time greatest action hero ever to walk the planet.

> We love to be around full-throttle people.

The Ultimate Action Hero

All during His life on earth, in every way, Jesus dared to live to the extreme. He defied the walls and barriers that hold so many in so tightly.

He was the best of friends; just ask Peter, James, and John. Or Lazarus and Mary and Martha.

He was as healthy as an ox; just ask the soldiers who had to put Him to death.

He was a brilliant thinker; just ask the teachers in the temple who were humbled by a twelve year-old, or the Pharisees and Sadducees who years later were stumped by His answers to the trick questions they threw at Him.

And He was above all a man after the heart of His Father; just ask anyone who was there at the Jordan River when heaven split and God spoke aloud.

Even in His dying, He set for us the perfect example of

the unlimited life. Above Him on the cross, they could have hung this sign: *Here dies a Man who knew what it means to live.*

Jesus squeezed every bit of life out of His thirty-three years on Planet Earth. Every day was spent to the hilt. Just read for yourself. Whether He was resting or praying or working, He did it all-out. For Him, there was no in-between, no average. He wouldn't accept a half-life.

And you don't have to either.

God designed you to enjoy life to the full. Just imagine it: a vibrant walk with God; relationships that are deeply meaningful and lasting; clear direction and vision for your future; and plenty of energy to accomplish it all! That's what unlimited living is all about.

But maybe you're saying, "Wait a minute. Can we really expect to get everything we hope for out of life? Isn't life more about reducing our expectations and just learning to get along with the way things work?" Maybe that's what you've been taught. For a long time, that's what I thought, too.

But Someone proved me wrong.

A Missing Piece?

Fortunately we've been left with an amazing script of Jesus' life. The four men who wrote about His days on earth have left us with a treasure of snapshots revealing His actions, stories, and teachings. The four Gospels are rich with detail.

Nearly half His life has been left as a mystery.

From them we gain a good picture of the extraordinary circumstances surrounding His birth and infancy, plus a brief but fascinating account of His impressive wisdom at age twelve, and then plenty of incisive detail about the three years of His ministry. And the final week of His life is recorded in almost blow-by-blow accounts.

But one chunk of time seems to be glaringly missing. What happened to the span of time between age twelve and age thirty?

That's eighteen years of Jesus' life with almost no record. Jesus died when He was thirty-three, which means nearly half His life has been left as a mystery. Not an insignificant part, either.

For most of us, a lot of important things tend to happen in that time span. These are the years when we determine who we'll become. We develop our worldview, our opinions of others, and our acceptance of ourselves. We establish the habits that follow us the rest of our lives. We make friends who become the fabric of our future decisions. Most impor- tant, we solidify our relationship with God.

If you were recapping the life of someone you know who's thirty-three or older, could you leave out their teenage, college, and early career days and still do their story justice? Yet in the accounts we have for Jesus, those same years are left blank. It's almost like starting a novel, reading the first chap- ter, then skipping to page 220. You would definitely feel you were missing something in the way of character development and plot progression.

Is it possible He went from age twelve to age thirty with- out any events of real consequence happening to Him? Not very likely. In fact, look closer at the Gospels and you'll see that we do get at least a glimpse into the haze of those miss- ing eighteen years—the years when He matured from a boy into a man, the years when His friends were getting married, the years when He followed in Joseph's footsteps and became a carpenter in Nazareth.

That glimpse we're given—more like a flash—is just one verse, Luke 2:52. In the verse before it, Jesus had just finished confounding the Pharisees in the temple as a twelve-year-old boy. And in the verse that comes after it (Luke 3:1), we launch into the account of John the Baptist at the time when Jesus begins His public ministry at age thirty.

Only one verse, one sentence. Here it is: "And Jesus grew in wisdom and stature, and in favor with God and men" (NIV).

The 252 Matrix

Look at the words closely. Jesus grew in *wisdom;* Jesus grew in *stature;* Jesus grew *in favor with God;* and Jesus grew *in favor with men*. Luke refers to four basic, distinct areas that are a part of all our lives, four spheres that make up the total picture of any person.

Wisdom makes us think of the mind, and of our strategy for living that we plan for and live out as we make choices. *Stature* recalls physical growth, our strength and health and energy. Growing *in favor with God* brings to mind our spirituality, and growing *in favor with men* encompasses all our human relationships.

And Luke tells us that in each of these four areas, Jesus *grew*. That's the operative word in Luke 2:52. It means He stretched His mind, His body, and His relationships, expanding Himself, pushing out of bounds. He was a picture of not only living a whole life, but fully engaging life and bursting limits. He made the effort to move from where He was to where He ended up.

We can call this fourfold look at life the 252 Matrix. With it, we see how Jesus gives us the perfect picture of a fully engaged life. As He matured and prepared for His life's calling, He wasn't satisfied to remain the same in any area, but actively increased in each one—physically, mentally, socially, and spiritually. And that's the same plan He has for us.

But is pushing forward in all four areas really that important? Can't we be totally happy and fulfill God's plan for our lives without thinking this broadly?

I don't think so, and here's why: For each of us, our life is bigger than we are. Ultimately, life's purpose is not about our happiness; after all, we don't even belong to ourselves. "You were bought at a price; therefore glorify God in your body and in your spirit, which are God's" (1 Corinthians 6:20, NKJV). We're God's instruments on earth, and He wants to get every ounce of impact from our lives—not for our sake, for our own ambition or personal glory, but for His sake.

Since our lives are not our own, we should strive to steward every moment, every emotion, and every ounce of energy for His kingdom. And we'll need all that, if we're going to accomplish His plan for our lives.

The goal of full engagement is not to become a neurotic Christian, constantly worried that you might be blowing it in one of the areas of your life. Rather, it's maintaining a mentality that says, "I want to steward every area of my life for the glory of God."

The Only Total Worship

A different aspect of these four areas shows up when Jesus was asked one day to identify the greatest commandment.

He answered this way: "'Love the Lord your God with all your heart and with all your soul and with all your strength and with all your mind'; and, 'Love your neighbor as yourself'" (Luke 10:27, NIV). Jesus emphasizes the importance of these crucial areas of life by encouraging us to *love God through each one*: through our heart and soul (the core within us, which always has to be our beginning spiritual point for growing in favor with God); through our strength (where we grow in stature, in physical vitality and energy); through our mind (where we understand wisdom and plan our life strategy); and through loving our neighbor as ourselves (which allows us to grow in favor with other people).

Full engagement is the greatest expression of total surrender to God.

And notice that Jesus asks us to love Him with *all* of our heart, soul, strength, and mind. That means 100 percent. Not 50 or 75 or even 98 percent, but with everything we are and have. Loving God is essentially worship, and God wants us to worship Him totally, extremely, and radically. That's full engagement, and it's the greatest expression of our absolute and total surrender to God.

Only a Balanced Life?

A few nights ago, Sarah and I went to a local restaurant and were talking over some of the ideas I'm developing in this book. We were served by a twenty-six-year-old waiter named Brent. He was dressed totally in black and had three rings in one ear and a bar through his tongue. A tribal tattoo stretched across his wrist and he wore a pair of hip black-rimmed glasses over his piercing blue eyes. As he refilled our water goblets, I asked him what he thought about living a "balanced life."

Immediately he replied, "Talk about boring! No way; life's too short."

You might say Brent sounds like a typical twentysomething who has nothing better to do than wait tables and waste his weekends. I might have said the same thing, too, had I not learned that he's working on his third master's degree and has big plans for his life, including running a youth surfing camp in California. Brent has dreams, but to him, life is an adventure to be lived, not an event to be planned. The last thing he wants to do is reduce his life to a chart and a script and a schedule. To him, a "balanced life" sounds like eating your vegetables and folding your underwear. It's like someone who's always telling you how to walk, how to talk, and what to wear, who pops up no matter which direction you turn.

No, the fully engaged life isn't about getting "balanced" by setting down rules and restrictions on every side. It's about turning in every direction and bursting free into the wild unknown.

Sputter Prevention

Dad and I made a deal: Straight A's in exchange for a car. So I was Einstein for a semester, and I knew exactly what vehicle I wanted. I had first spied the 1986 CJ7 Jeep in a used car lot on my way home from school one day. It was a few years old, but it was the exact body style and color I was looking for. Sleek black, 32-inch tires, and a ragtop. So I got it. It was to be, as my sisters called it, my "babe magnet." It looked great and it ran like a dream. Well, at least most of the time.

I was driving my Jeep one day when I heard a terrible noise. The vehicle suddenly jerked forward and began to chug and sputter and choke. I discovered that one of the cylinders in the engine had gone bad. It threw the entire Jeep out of whack.

That's a good picture of what happens when one aspect of the 252 Matrix isn't operating like it should. Life works smoothest when all four elements of the 252 Matrix are working together. God created us as four-part people, and to neglect one of the parts can be harmful to our ability to fulfill our life's mission.

I know a guy whose relationship with God seems totally

dialed in, plus he exercises every day and has a lot of great friends. But he hasn't put his mind to work to develop a God-breathed strategy or vision for his life. Rather than assessing his skills and using the incredible intellect God gave him (he has a Harvard degree), he senses a lack of direction and blames others around him for it. He tells me that he'll just "know" one day what he's supposed to do with his life.

Then there's a woman I know who's great at planning the details of her life—it's all scripted from beginning to end. God seems to be in His rightful place in her heart, and the right friends are in place, too. Everything's going along just fine—except that she isn't physically fit and lacks energy. She'd be amazed at how much more she could accomplish if she took time to better steward her health.

You get the picture. What good does it really do you if your body's in great shape but your relationships are a wreck? Or how valuable is your life if you have great friends and good health and a strong career path, but you're hardly on speaking terms with God?

It's true that some men and women seem to achieve a measure of apparent success without developing every element of the 252 Matrix, but they're selling themselves short. When all four aspects are being fully engaged—when we're operating with all four cylinders running at full throttle—we experience more fulfillment, more opportunity, and more energy than we otherwise would ever know.

Most of us tend to assume we're quite capable of developing two or maybe even three areas of the 252 Matrix with little or no help. But without total surrender to God, it's impossible to fully develop according to God's standards in even one of these areas, let alone engage all four.

Maybe you can think of someone who's been noticeably failing to grow and expand in one or more of those four spheres of the 252 Matrix. Maybe that someone is you.

Or maybe for you it's not so much a case of outright failure in one or more areas, but of simply needing encouragement and help to more faithfully expand in each aspect by God's grace. If that's you, then keep reading, because that encouragement and help is on the way. And it comes first in the form of a good long look at all the characters who play a part in the epic story that is your life.

Your Takeaway

Plot Points

- You're called to live to the extreme—to be fully engaged—in every area of your life.
- This kind of fully engaged living is required for you to accomplish your God-given mission and to make the most of your God-given freedom.
- Jesus was a model for us in growing in every area of His life.
- In Luke 2:52 we find a model for evaluating our life-growth in every area—in the *mental* realm, including our wisdom and strategy for living; in the *physical* realm, particularly in health and energy; in the *spiritual* realm with our relationship with God; and in the *social* realm with our relationships with other people.

Dialogue with a Sage

- Why are you convinced that it's important to be fully engaged—developing in all four areas of the 252 Matrix?

- Have you allowed yourself to put any of these areas on the back burner? If so, what can you do to change that?
- At what time in your past did you feel most alive? What caused you to feel this way?

From the Script

"And you must love the Lord your God with all your heart, all your soul, all your mind, and all your strength" (Mark 12:30).

part**two**

THE
CHARACTERS

chapter six

THE UNSUSPECTING HERO

Your Time for Action

A few weeks ago, I woke up and saw a light coming from under the door of the boys' room. As I walked closer, the commotion behind the door sounded like the equivalent of the South Stands at a Broncos football game.

They must have heard me coming. Before I could turn the handle, the door swung open. "We're good pirates! Give us your money!"

I looked down and saw Harrison and Chandler standing there, dressed in the full plastic armor they'd just gotten for Christmas. Chandler's outfit was at least two sizes too big, and he was at a clear disadvantage to his brother, since it was obvious he couldn't see a thing.

My two boys held up their swords and delivered their threat: I was to go to their castle or else the dragon would get me. Of course, I went to the castle.

As I sat on Harrison's bed, I knew I needed a way to escape the dragon, so I opted for a distraction. I asked the boys what they wanted to be when they got big. That seemed to capture their thoughts for a moment.

"I want to be a soldier and a fireman and Spider-Man," Harrison answered.

I turned to Chandler. "Peter Pan" was his answer.

Typical boys, you say. Typical people, I say. Deep inside, we all long to live a life of significance where we get to be a hero.

The Deepest Desperation

In 1845, naturalist Henry David Thoreau packed his bags and trudged into the woods around Walden Pond in Massachusetts. He lived there alone for three years, determined to find himself. Actually, he was determined to find life.

"I went to the woods," he later wrote in *Walden*, "because I wished to live deliberately, to front only the essential facts of life, and see if I could not learn what it had to teach, and not, when I came to die, to discover that I had not lived. I did not wish to live what was not life, living is so dear."

It was Thoreau who also observed that "most men lead lives of quiet desperation." This desperation is something like a deep, inward desire for a life beyond the one you're living. You go about your daily routines, all the while knowing there's something more in you waiting to be set free.

The Hero Inside

I still remember standing in front of the Indian Hills movie theater in Omaha, Nebraska, when I was fifteen years old. I was with my best friend, Jeff Abboud, waiting in a line that seemed to stretch around the block. We finally found our seats near the front of the theater as the lights dimmed and *Raiders of the Lost Ark* began. I was mesmerized. Heroism, adventure, romance, spirituality. A life full of excitement, challenge, and risk. Since then, Indiana Jones has been my symbol of an adventurous life. (My oldest son's name is Harrison; my dog's is Indiana.)

Indiana Jones never called himself a hero. A true hero never does. He may know it, deep down inside, but he never says it.

> You'll probably be floored when God comes calling.

Then there are the heroes who have no idea what's really in them. That's most of us. Have you ever felt totally, absolutely, and completely incompetent and underqualified to do the things you believe you're supposed to do? Have you ever wondered if God has confused you with someone else? If you have, you're not alone.

At the core, nearly every epic story has an unsuspecting hero who, before the adventure begins, is just quietly living his life. Neo, the cyberaction hero of *The Matrix,* was a computer programmer before being told he's "the one" who can rescue the world. Or consider the unlikely heroes of our childhood comic books—so often they're the rejects and the outcasts.

What does the hero look like in the twenty-first century? The twentysomething girl working at Starbucks. The college student poring over philosophy books. The middle-aged man working as an accountant. These are the unsuspecting heroes. These are the Neos whom God is looking for today, the people destined for an unlimited life.

Chances are that means *you* are a candidate. And if history is any indication, you'll probably be floored when God comes calling.

Mighty Warrior

I wonder if Gideon ever saw it coming.

What a scene it must have been. The people of God had

once again been scared into the hills. The Midianites and their allies were camped in the valley of Jezreel, swarming like flies, nearly 150,000 strong. Everyone knew this valley belonged to the Israelites, but that didn't matter to these guys. For seven years they'd been repeatedly raiding Israel and pillaging homes, crops, and livestock, and they weren't about to stop now.

The Israelites were scared to death. Under such fierce oppression, most had scattered and were living in caves and hideouts up in the rugged mountains above the valley. And they cried out to the Lord. In the dead of night, among the dark shadows inside their caves, they must have lain awake and groaned, "Why is all this happening to us? Where are You, God, when we need You most? Aren't we Your chosen people?"

A man named Gideon felt the same despair and fear that gripped his countrymen. When it was time to thresh wheat, he'd gone inside a winepress, where his work and the precious grain would be out of sight—to keep it from falling into the enemy's hands like everything else.

Suddenly, Gideon noticed someone seated under a tree just outside the winepress. His stomach must have nearly pushed itself through his throat. Was it an enemy?

But the stranger quickly said, "The Lord is with you, mighty warrior."

So this wasn't an enemy after all, but someone bringing God's message to Gideon. And what was Gideon's first response to this affirmation, to these words that were probably the greatest compliment he'd ever received? Did he fall to his knees? Did he shout, "Hallelujah"? Did he cover his face with his hands and weep? Hardly. The stranger's words about the Lord's presence unleashed the heavy questions every Israelite had been harboring, and Gideon let them gush out:

"Sir," Gideon replied, "if the LORD is with us, why has all this happened to us? And where are all the miracles our ancestors told us about? Didn't they say, 'The LORD brought us up out of Egypt'? But now the LORD has abandoned us and handed us over to the Midianites." (Judges 6:13)

With that kind of reaction from Gideon, I suppose God could have just turned to go try out the next guy. He might even have struck Gideon with a bolt of lightning. Or He could simply have disappeared from Israel forever and forgotten about rescuing these annoying people.

But God was unfazed by Gideon's frustration. I think He even liked Gideon's transparency.

Then the LORD turned to him and said, "Go with the strength you have and rescue Israel from the Midianites. I am sending you!" (6:14)

I'm sure Gideon couldn't help looking over his shoulder: *Who, me?* Had he heard this visitor right? *You're God, and You're asking me to rescue Israel from the swarms of soldiers down there? Yeah, right.*

Somehow, though, this stranger seemed serious. So Gideon once again showed his true colors, being perfectly honest about how he felt:

"But Lord," Gideon replied, "how can I rescue Israel? My clan is the weakest in the whole tribe of Manasseh, and I am the least in my entire family!" (6:15)

Was God only joking? No, He wasn't. This was the real deal.

God's Cue

I know exactly how Gideon felt.

The phone rang one day in 1995, and my pastor, Ted Haggard, casually invited me to travel with him to Tulsa, Oklahoma. We were going to scout out some students at Oral Roberts University as candidates in our search for a new youth pastor at our church. I knew lots of people at ORU, so I accepted.

On our way to Tulsa, we were walking down a corridor at the airport in Dallas when it hit me. For reasons I still don't fully understand, I turned to Pastor Ted as we were walking and said, "I think I might be God's third or fourth choice for this, but if you'll have me, I'd be honored to be your new youth pastor."

Pastor Ted jokingly asked me why I hadn't told him a few hours earlier. And so, within a few weeks, I was preparing for my first youth meeting.

On the day before it was scheduled, I crossed the street in front of our apartment building and wandered into a field where I liked to go and pray. It was my winepress. I paced and prayed and tried to preach to the rocks scattered across the field. I pictured the room at the church with a scattered group of students, waiting to hear from their new youth pastor. And suddenly I was scared to death. My mouth dried up, my heart was pounding out of my chest, and I felt sick to my stomach.

"I'm not the guy!" I told God. "I made a mistake. I jumped the gun. I'm not sup-posed to be doing this." I just didn't feel like youth pastor material. After all, I'd never spoken in front of a church group in my life, and I'd never taken a class in youth ministry or preaching or any-thing remotely close to it. I was a businessman, not a pastor. *I'm not even a very spiritual guy,* I thought.

> "I'm not the guy!"
> I told God.

All my weaknesses and faults and vices were glaring at me. I wanted to run.

"No, I'm not the one!" I said out loud. "I'm the last guy who should be doing this."

And I think that's exactly what God wanted to hear. He was looking for an unsuspecting hero. That was the moment God was waiting for.

The Hero Maker

As God kept affirming His surprising message for Gideon, it made Gideon feel more than ever like a weakling. Yet when he admitted he was only the least of his family, it was God's cue to let Gideon know, *"I'll* be right there with you—and *that's* why you'll succeed." God kept seeing him as a hero because *He Himself* would be with Gideon to *make* him a hero:

> The LORD said to him, "I will be with you. And you will destroy the Midianites as if you were fighting against one man." (6:16)

There's the paradox again of the unlimited life. You have to be the least to be the greatest. God isn't looking for those who think they have it all together. He isn't necessarily looking for the ones who look the part and say all the right things. His eyes aren't focused on people with shining résumés and killer endorsements. He's looking for the Frodos and the Neos and the Gideons—the men and women willing to wear their heart on their sleeve and come honestly to the King. He's searching for those who understand that outside of God, it's all impossible.

With Gideon, God chose a scared, paranoid leader, and he and his band of men soundly defeated their enemy against what must have been the greatest odds in military history: 150,000 to 300.

And for me, on the day I was praying in that field across from our apartment, when I felt totally unprepared and unequipped to do the task laid out ahead of me, when I felt weak and needed something to hold onto...God took that frightened, sketchy youth-pastor-to-be and used him to help raise up a vibrant youth ministry with global impact.

That's just the way God is.

"Go with the strength you have," He says. "I'm sending *you!*" That was God's message for Gideon, and it's His message for us.

The epic adventure He's planned for us begins with a willing but unsuspecting hero. Maybe, like Gideon, you find yourself looking over your shoulder. *Who, me? You must be kidding.* It's fine to be transparent. That's what God wants from us. But face up to the truth: God is calling you to an unlimited adventure, a heroic life.

Made for This Moment

And it's a life He's perfectly shaped you for. He created you for this very moment in time...and there's never been anyone quite like you.

God created you absolutely unique. He designed you with a distinct personality pattern that's unlike anyone else's. He masterfully engineered you before you were ever born. Every freckle. Every hair. Every part of you. He knew exactly what He wanted out of your life. The Bible says He actually chose us "before the foundation of the world" (Ephesians 1:4, NKJV). Regardless of what you may think, you weren't an accident. That's an impossibility for God. He never makes mistakes. You were carefully and thoughtfully planned out well before you ever began to breathe. He formed you with your likes and dislikes, your passions and dreams...to accomplish *His* purpose in your life.

You are the hero of your epic because you have a unique place in God's story. No one else can do what you were designed to do. You aren't a bystander in your story...you're the central figure. That's how God made it for all of us. And "his divine power gives us everything we need" to live out that story through a godly life (2 Peter 1:3).

So why, like Gideon, do we hide out in the winepress? Have we forgotten how much our Creator loves us?

So many people in our generation are asking the same haunting questions the Israelites asked thousands of years ago: "Where's God now that I need Him the most? Where's my freedom and fulfillment? Why are all these problems happening in my life?"

But in the dark caves of our Christian subculture where we've retreated, God is calling us once again to come out. He's waiting to assure us that He'll be with us every step of the way, and He'll forever stay true to His promise: "Never will I leave you; never will I forsake you" (Hebrews 13:5, NIV).

With You

My son Harrison started playing T-ball when he was three years old. To give him extra help, I bought a cheap T-ball set at Wal-Mart and we practiced in our backyard. I knew he could hit the ball, and I knew he could run.

Then came time for his first game. At a soggy baseball field across the street from the YMCA, a couple dozen of us parents were gathered, looking out on our prized little ones who were no taller than the bats they were using.

It was the Red Team versus the Yellow Team. Harrison

was number 4 for the Reds, and his turn to bat finally came. He walked up to the tee. After three or four or five strikes, he connected.

I was so excited I ran right along with him from first base all the way back to home plate. I cheered at the top of my lungs the entire way around the field. "Come on, Harrison! You can do it! Just one more base!"

I loved it. I loved watching him do what I knew he could do.

And so does God.

He's watching now from the sidelines as you come up to bat, so glad that instead of

> God loves watching us do what He knows we can do.

sitting behind the fence, you've accepted the challenge He created you for. And as you race around the bases, He can't help but run alongside and call out to you, "Come on! I know you can do it! That's how I made you!"

God thoroughly understands the gap between where you are and where you could be…and so He'll be with you all the way as you shorten that distance.

Your Hour, Your Battle

The enemy is camped in the valley of our culture, and it's time for you to accept God's personal call to battle. How long will you wait while the enemy steals from us? How long will you stand by as he assaults our generation with lies and perversion and artificial passion? It's time for you to stop waiting for the strength and to start standing up when God calls.

Yes, mighty warrior, that's you He's talking to. Stop looking over your shoulder and shrugging it away.

Accept your calling as one of God's heroes. It's time to get ready for the battle ahead.

Plot Points

- God is looking for unsuspecting heroes—those who are honest about their shortcomings and realistic about their desperate dependence on Him.
- God created you with everything you need to be the hero of your chapter in His story. He created you in every way to fulfill His purpose through you.
- His presence with you will give you the strength and all the resources you need for accomplishing His purpose for your life.

Dialogue with a Sage

- How did you first come to realize God's call on your life?
- In what ways have you struggled with insecurity or felt inadequate to do what God called you to do?
- Is it easy for you to embrace the idea of being the hero in the God-inspired epic that's your life?
- What characteristics make you the perfect hero in your particular epic?
- Do you face any mental barriers to believing that God wants to do a great work in and through your life?

From the Script

"For we are God's masterpiece. He has created us anew in Christ Jesus, so that we can do the good things he planned for us long ago" (Ephesians 2:10).

chapter seven

THE VILLAIN

Your Enemy Is Real

 Something woke me up this morning at 2:00 A.M. I heard the toilet flush in the bathroom, then the sound of little feet walking back down the hallway.

Then I noticed. He'd left the light on...*again.*

A bit frustrated, I flipped the sheets over, stumbled out of bed and down the hall. I reached my hand around the wall of the bathroom to turn off the lights. "At least he flushed," I thought as I walked back to our room. That's when I heard a quiet voice. "Daddy, come here." He must have seen me.

"It's okay, Harrison, go back to sleep."

"Daddy, please."

I'm a sucker. I walked back to the boys' room. Chandler was fast asleep, sprawled out upside down and half naked, with a water gun still in his hands (obviously sneaked into bed after stories and prayers). Harrison was sitting up in the corner of his bed with the covers pulled up to his chest. In the moonlight filtering through the window, I could see his eyes. He was scared.

Monsters

For an instant, all the nightmares of my own childhood came racing back. I used to have this one recurring dream of Chaka from *The Planet of the Apes* chasing me around the outside of my grandparents' house. And I remembered what it was like to stare at my stuffed animals, swearing they'd just moved.

I quietly slipped into bed next to Harrison and rested my head on the pillow next to his. For a moment, we both lay there, quietly looking at the light and shadows mixing together on the ceiling of his room.

"What are you afraid of?" I asked as casually as I could.

"Well, I know there aren't any monsters," he said, only half-convinced. "But I'm just a little bit afraid of the dark."

> There is such a thing as monsters.

"It's okay," I assured him. "I used to be a bit scared when I was a little boy, too."

"You did?" he said, as if there was no possible way his dad could ever be afraid of anything. After all, I'm the one who could beat up the Incredible Hulk, Superman, and Samson, all at the same time—or at least that's what I'd overheard the boys saying a few days earlier.

"Dad?" Harrison said in a half-question, half-statement. "I love you." He reached over and slid his hand around my arm. That was that. Neither of us said anything else. For a long time, we just lay there looking at the ceiling until we both fell asleep.

I wanted to tell Harrison there wasn't anything to worry about. That there was no such thing as monsters. But I knew that isn't true.

Your Archenemy

Pollsters report that lots of us (even so-called Christians) believe there's no such thing as the devil. But just take a walk through Blockbuster Video. Or turn on your TV. Nearly any night of the week, you can have your pick of the under-world—for starters, there's *Buffy the Vampire Slayer, The X-Files, The Outer Limits, Charmed,* and *Haunted.*

There's a reason we're so curious about all this. It's more real than lots of us like to admit.

Don't be fooled, the devil is alive and well. And he's the archenemy of the epic life. He's the villain in our story, and the greatest threat against you.

Of course he doesn't take on the form of a cape-wearing ghoul with horns, a pointed tail, and bad makeup. No, he's smarter than that. And it's high time we wise up. If we're ever going to break through the things that limit us, we've got to face up to the one who posts the signs and sets up the barriers to begin with.

Paul talked about making sure "that Satan will not out-smart us," and about being "very familiar with his evil schemes" (2 Corinthians 2:11). This enemy is no idiot. Quite the opposite: He's cunning, crafty, and relentlessly cruel.

Basically, we can summarize his attributes under three names for him: He's the accuser, he's the deceiver, and he's the tempter. And in those roles, the three primary weapons in his arsenal are guilt, fear, and greed. Everything he throws at you can be traced to these three, in one way or another.

Let's uncover more about his tactics so you can outsmart him, as Paul says, and not let him sidetrack you from fulfill-ing your greatest potential.

The Accuser

A man sits alone in an office with a .45 clenched in his hands.

A girl sobs as she remembers giving away her virginity.

A young man forces down another drink, trying to forget

his careless words and his mother's wounded look.

And the voice of the accuser begins to ring in their heads: "You'll never change. You've already messed up too much. You've hurt too many people. God can't stand you. You've gone too far. Remember what you did? Remember? Remember?"

The words have echoed in humanity's ears for thousands of years. We started listening in the garden and we've never stopped.

God created Adam and Eve to be free and never told them otherwise, even after the Fall. And yet the enemy's accusation was so piercing that within minutes they were running scared, ducking away from God in shame. "What have you done?" the accuser whispered. "He'll never forgive you. And—oh my gosh!—you're naked!"

So where do we find Adam after he sinned? Seeking after God? Falling to his knees? Hardly. He was hiding in the underbrush, covering himself with leaves.

And when God confronted him, Adam replied, "I heard you, so I hid. I was afraid because I was naked." God then asked Adam, "Who told you that you were naked?" (Genesis 3:10–11). But of course, God knew all too well the answer.

In the Scriptures, the Greek word for "devil" is *diabolos,* which literally means "accuser." That's his name. He's the one who accused Adam, and the same battle goes on today, with guilt as the weapon of choice.

Unfair Fighting

For Satan to use guilt is unfair fighting—below the belt and against the rules in every way. Satan himself is more guilty than anyone else God has ever created. But then, Satan never has played by the rules. He knows the future belongs to God, so he's figured out how to use our own stale, forgotten past against us.

But it's a ruse. An illusion. Once we've been to the cross, his accusations hold no water. And yet he keeps on accusing, day after day, reminding, prodding, mocking. It's time for you and me to turn, look him in the face, and remind him of Christ's work at Calvary.

That's where Jesus took all of it—all our guilt. On the cross, the King of kings "was counted among those who were sinners" (Isaiah 53:12). The ultimate trade-off. He assumed *our* guilt. "All of us have strayed away like sheep. We have left God's paths to follow our own. Yet *the LORD laid on him the guilt and sins of us all*" (53:6, italics mine). Jesus took on *all* of it in one incredible moment…and gave us His pure righteousness in exchange.

Just ask the thief who was given access that same day into paradise—slate wiped clean. Once and for all.

Fortunately, we know how Satan's story ends. We know what will happen, in the moment all of heaven is waiting for: "Then I heard a loud voice shouting across the heavens, 'It has happened at last—the salvation and power and kingdom of our God, and the authority of his Christ! For the Accuser has been thrown down to earth—the one who accused our brothers and sisters before our God day and night'" (Revelation 12:10).

The enemy will get his just rewards. Rest assured, he'll pay the ultimate price. God will get His vengeance.

But until then, keep your eyes open and remember: Your sins will either draw you closer to God and your potential in Him as you embrace His forgiveness with repentance and praise, or they'll pull you away from Him if you let Satan trap you with guilt. It's up to you.

Jesus calls the devil "a liar and the father of lies" (John 8:44). He continues sowing his seeds of deceit, which bear fruit in lie after lie after lie—white lies, black lies, and every possible twisting of the truth.

The devil knows exactly what buttons to push to make his lies believable to us. He'll often do it in a way that seems harmless—"as an angel of light," which is the way he disguises himself (2 Corinthians 11:14). But his lies about your life and your future will lead you down the slippery path and eventually to the death of your dream, your vision, and your passion.

One of the devil's favorite forms of deception is the enemy called average—the belief that average is enough, that there's no real reason for pressing the limits, that it's better to be comfortable than to be free. Like the producer in *The Truman Show,* the enemy would love for us to spend the rest of our lives running on average rather than running free.

> Satan corners us with fear.

In the Garden, the father of lies deceived Eve into believing what was essentially the mother of all lies—that we can be like God. Satan knows how enticing this is. He knows how easily we'll go for it. Once we do, we try to build our own lives, and we make the mistake of trying to succeed without God. When we start recognizing that we aren't going to be able to pull it off, that's when Satan pulls his punch. He corners us with fear. Fear of failure. Fear of what others will think and say about us. Even fear of punishment from God.

My dog Indiana is a digger—especially in my neighbors' yards. After more than a year of phone calls from them, I decided to do something about it. I put up an invisible fence, which is actually a metal wire buried a few inches in the ground. Indiana wears a small electric receiver on his collar that gives him a mild shock every time he gets too close to the invisible barrier. Fear is just like that. It can hold you in a vise grip that effectively stops you from making any forward progress in the direction of your goals.

But there's hope. Paul says it's possible to "escape from the Devil's trap," even for people who "have been held captive by him to do whatever he wants" (2 Timothy 2:26). How do we escape the devil's trap when he grips us with fear? We do what every great hero does—we face that fear.

That's what I did a few years ago. Although I never wanted to admit it, fear had become an unwanted companion. Now, I'm a pretty secure guy at heart. Anyone who knows me will quickly tell you I'm optimistic, positive, and self-confident. I'm not afraid of the future, I'm not afraid of challenges, and I'm certainly not afraid of risk. The brand of fear that had gripped me was something else, and it's the worst kind—a fear of people.

What will they think? What if I let them down? What if they react? What if they reject me? That's what I kept wondering. So I found myself shrinking back when I should have been pressing on. I found myself more concerned about the opinions of others than the opinion of God. I had ideas in ministry and business that I'd abandoned simply because others thought they were foolish. I avoided any potential conflicts with people, and I can't tell you how many times I found myself carefully watching every word so I wouldn't offend or turn off anyone around me.

I'd become so bound up in my fear that I began to believe this was just the way I am. The deceiver had me convinced I would never change. Fortunately, a few good friends rallied around me to help. They convinced me the best weapon I had was action. I had to face the thing that had been "stealing my strength," as John Eldredge puts it. I did. And when I did, I began to get my strength back, slowly but surely. Fear was replaced with a confidence and strength I'd never known before.

The Tempter

As the tempter, the devil's most potent weapon against you is greed—and not just for money. Greed, essentially, is the temptation to get more than you need of something. We can be greedy for more power or more attention as well as for more things or more wealth.

We learn greed almost as soon as we can walk. Harrison always wants what Chandler has and Chandler always wants what Harrison has. And when one of them drops the thing in their hands to pick up something else, the new thing suddenly becomes the most important thing in the world. We get older and the things change, but the story is basically the same.

Today I went to the gym to run on the treadmill. I usually try to work out in the morning before the day gets going, but today I was a bit off schedule and my workout came at about two o'clock in the afternoon. I jumped onto the treadmill and realized I'd forgotten my headphones, which I usually use to tune into CNN on one of the television screens lined up in front of the exercise machines. As I started running, I couldn't help but glance from screen to screen, trying to make sense out of the flashing images without hearing the words. One of the screens flashed the word *Passions*. That got my attention.

It was a soap opera. I'd never heard of this program, but it wasn't too difficult to follow along with, even without words. The storyline went something like this: In one situation, a young couple, clearly just finished making love, were fighting (overdone tears and a thrown bottle were the clues) over what I'm guessing was another woman. A drawn-out scuffle in a dark, fuzzy room followed the bottle incident. Then the drama switched to a scene on a balcony somewhere. Another fight, this time apparently over someone's inheritance. Angry words. More angry words. Then a few fists. Finally, a girl lay dead on the deck. (The actress will probably come back next season as the twin.)

Back to the first scene. Now the man is with a different woman (the cause of the bottle fight, I'm assuming). The encounter quickly leads to a made-for-TV love scene and fades out.

Back to the balcony. Two men are dragging the body out of the room and into a car, clearly hiding the evidence that will probably be uncovered in tomorrow's episode.

And so it went. The program seemed to be replete with deceit, envy, greed, and lust (what they call "passion").

As I finished my run, my head was spinning. Life in general may not be as sensational as a soap opera makes it, but the attacks we face from the villain are just as tragic and ugly and real.

Our Weapons

Those attacks are everywhere. In our offices and in our homes and churches, the devil targets men and women, old and young, with guilt, fear, and greed.

It would be easy to get discouraged, shrink back, and try to play it safe. But then, that's not the way God fights; and it's not the way *we* fight when we join with Him in battle. "We use God's mighty weapons, not mere worldly weapons, to knock down the Devil's strongholds" (2 Corinthians 10:4).

Yes, we have weapons, too—the Word of God, the Holy Spirit alive in us, and worship, to name a few.

So don't just lay back and stare at the ceiling, wondering if there are monsters in your life. There are. Now take up your weapons and prepare for the war.

Your Takeaway

Plot Points

- Satan—the villain in your epic story—is real and is actively working to thwart God's plan for your life.
- To defeat the villain, you must understand how he works.
- Your enemy operates especially as the accuser, the deceiver, and the tempter.
- Three of your enemy's chief weapons are guilt, fear, and greed.

Dialogue with a Sage

- How have you most often seen the enemy's attacks in your life?
- What are the most effective ways for us to respond to the enemy's attacks?
- What do you think the accuser is most likely to accuse you of? What will he try to make you feel guilty for?
- What is the deceiver most likely to try deceiving you about? What will he try to make you fear?
- What is the tempter most likely to tempt you with? What will he try to make you greedy for?
- What will you have to do to defeat the villain in each of these areas?

From the Script

Jesus said, "The thief's purpose is to steal and kill and destroy" (John 10:10).

chapter eight

THE KING

The Hero Maker

ere's something to understand as a foundation for everything else in this book: The call to Life Unlimited is transcended by the call of the cross.

Jesus isn't just an example of greatness; He *is* greatness. To fully pursue a life without limits, we've got to first pursue and follow the One who's limitless. The only reason we can be a hero is because He is *the* Hero, first and last. And He proved it on Calvary.

King of the Hill

For a kid, there's nothing quite like a construction site. When I was ten years old, a new house was being built in our neighborhood, and I remember wandering onto the building site with my buddies Ricky and Mike. We weren't allowed to be there, of course, but that was beside the point and all the more reason to duck under the plastic tape and walk around the lot.

For a while, we were content to walk around the half-finished house, discovering a few treasures—a broken hammer, several dozen unused nails, two half-empty tubes of caulking. Then we spotted the hill. To the average passerby it was only a mound of dirt waiting to be moved or leveled. But to us, it was an ideal site for a battle. It was the perfect mound of dirt for a game of king of the hill.

You know the game. One person takes to the top of the hill and the others try to dethrone him, until only one prevails. You can see the picture. Three boys shouting, tugging, pulling, pushing their way to the top, throwing one another off, and the process repeated endlessly.

Now imagine another picture.

Three grown men nailed to crosses on the top of a very different hill. Their shouting is not yelling for fun, but cries of pain. They're not tugging at one another's arms and shirts; they're straining against the nails holding them to the wood.

This isn't the place where boys assert their pride; it's the place where the King of the universe asserts His love in order to save the world.

Jesus was the ultimate mold breaker. His life was full of upstream swimming and going against the grain. He, who was worthy of any and every throne, found Himself instead on a lonely hillside riveted to an old rugged cross. The King of kings was willing to become the King of the hill. For us.

That hill, that mound of dirt and rock called Calvary, is the place where God Himself decided to exchange all His wonder and innocence and humility for all our ambition and greed and pride. It was more than an execution site. It was the staging ground for the climax of an eternal drama.

And it's here at Calvary that the epic life begins. It's what gives meaning to each of our stories. Jesus said, "If you try to keep your life for yourself, you will lose it. But if you give up your life for me, you will find true life" (Matthew 16:25). The cross was, for a moment, the throne of God. The King gave His life so that ours could have real meaning. The cross gave us something to die for. Even more, it gave us something to live for—and to stay connected with.

That's where it gets hard.

Misdirected

A few months ago, I was up to my shoulders directing *The Thorn,* an annual Easter production we've staged at our church each spring for the past eight years. The production is massive, with a cast of over four hundred and a movie-style set. *The Thorn* attracts over thirty thousand people every year, and this was shaping up to be our best year ever. Everything was in place and moving along like clockwork. The devil's makeup and costuming was terrifying. The angels were incredible, complete with new swords and special effects. We'd added a revolving set that was working like a dream.

I was in my element. Typically during those months I sleep little, drink too much Starbucks, and move a hundred miles an hour. I wasn't prepared for my world to fall apart. One afternoon, while I was working on the set, I got a phone call from Jesus. Actually, it was from my good friend Mark Russell, who has played the part of Jesus in *The Thorn* ever since I first wrote the script eight years ago. Mark told me he was struggling with his role and wasn't going to be able to play the part.

I didn't know what to say. Mark knew the part backward and forward. He was the most believable Jesus I'd ever worked with or even seen for that matter. And to top it all off, we were only two weeks from opening night. I went through the roof.

The next day, I held Jesus auditions, which didn't help the way I felt. I selected James Bennett, Mark's understudy, to play the main role, and he quickly dove into the part, working hard to get it right.

The next two weeks were hell for me. Everything seemed to fall apart. Our lighting board was out of commission, John the Baptist nearly quit, every actor had an opinion contrary to mine, an angel had to get thirty stitches after being cut by a demon, and the devil was beginning to lose his face, literally. And because *The Thorn* was my baby, I went into overdrive to fix it. I worked harder, later, and more furiously than ever.

> I should have heard the enemy laughing.

I should have heard him laughing. The enemy had directed my heart away from the real purpose of *The Thorn,* and he was winning. The villain was using ministry as a distraction from Him.

One night after rehearsal, I was sitting at a restaurant at midnight and it hit me. *The Thorn* wasn't about me or a performer or sets or makeup or any of that. It was about Jesus. Simply Jesus.

Fortunately, God arrested me just in time. At the next rehearsal, we had a powerful prayer time. We repented for taking the reins, and we gave the show back to God.

This has been the most impacting year for *The Thorn* we've ever had. Had I missed God's cue, I would never have been aware of my shifting heart and would have put a lid on the unlimited possibilities God intended for me.

In Small Ways, Too

The same misdirection happens in small ways every day. Have you ever noticed how easy it is for your mind to drift as soon as you sit down to read the Bible? Doesn't it drive you crazy how your thoughts go off into the hinterlands when you begin a dialogue with God?

Just yesterday, I was driving to Denver and decided to fill the hour-long trip with worship. I popped my Passion music CD into the player and prepared to sing my guts out as I sped up the road. For some reason, the CD I'd been listening to all week wouldn't play. So I decided to pray instead. Suddenly I felt as though I was on a blind date with God. I fidgeted with the steering wheel as I prayed, and within a couple of minutes I ran out of things to say. I'm embarrassed to say I used the lull in the conversation to turn on the local Christian radio station, and I convinced myself it was nearly the same as worship.

How could that happen? I have a moment alone with the Creator of the universe, and I blow it with a few catchy Christian lyrics. Was that just a result of my boredom and lack of spiritual maturity, or was it something more? Could it be I was undergoing a massive battle for my heart and I didn't even know it? Could it be the enemy saw a potential power encounter with the King coming my way and threw everything he could at me to distract me into what was more comfortable?

It can happen so easily in every area of our lives: Something takes our eyes off God. It can be a new car or a new friend. A hobby can quickly take the King's place in our lives, and so can religious work. The last thing the enemy wants is for you to live in the fullness of life God designed for you, and he'll use whatever he can as an excuse to fill your days with anything less.

We've been warned: "Be careful! Watch out for attacks from the Devil, your great enemy. He prowls around like a roaring lion, looking for some victim to devour" (1 Peter 5:8).

Jesus called him a thief, and told us, "The thief's purpose is to steal and kill and destroy" (John 10:10). He's always the master of misdirection, constantly seeking to keep the King out of our focus, and to make us think we're in control.

Not Our Copilot

The other day I saw a bumper sticker that said, "God is my copilot." That's embarrassing. If God is my copilot, then that means I'm trying to be the pilot, and that's a ridiculous way to live. The last thing we want to do is take the steering wheel of our lives away from God and tell Him He can hold the map and point out directions and tell us where the next McDonald's is.

Remember, your life can be unlimited only to the degree that it's also surrendered. And that kind of surrender means you've got to be willing to die.

Remember in *The Princess Bride* when the old doctor, the Billy Crystal character, is asked to revive Wesley, the film's hero? Assessing the body, the doctor concludes that Wesley isn't dead, but "only mostly dead." That's a picture of what a lot of Christians are trying to be—half surrendered to God, and half holding on to their own lives.

Jesus doesn't want us to be half-dead Christians; He wants us to die fully to ourselves, then live fully in Him. Paul sets the example: "I myself no longer live, but *Christ lives in me*. So I live my life in this earthly body by trusting in the Son of God, who loved me and gave himself for me" (Galatians 2:20, italics mine).

> That's when supernatural synergy is ignited.

When we're connected with God in the truest sense of our affections and attention, then a supernatural synergy is born. As long as we attempt to live our own lives and pilot our own ship, we'll be limited to our human strength and willpower to get things done. But when we submit to God and refocus our attention onto Him, supernatural synergy is ignited. That's when we can say with Paul, "I can do all things through Christ who strengthens me" (Philippians 4:13, NKJV). Not through my own strength; not by merely thinking positive thoughts or repeating a nice mantra; but only through the King.

At the Controls

A few days ago, my good friend Barry took me for a ride in his plane. I sat next to him in the cockpit as we headed up over Colorado's Front Range and on toward Aspen. Right at about fifteen thousand feet, Barry asked me if I'd like to fly the plane.

Did he mean that? I thought. *Fly the plane?* "Of course I would!" I said. Barry instructed me to grab the copilot's yoke (the steering wheel). For the next few minutes, I was flying. Or at least I thought I was. I was carefully tapping the yoke as Barry instructed, gently moving from one position to the next.

I felt like a bird, and I looked over at the pilot and he was smiling from ear to ear. He was loving watching me fly. Then, for a moment, I looked down at the instruments on the control panel. When I looked back up, we were quickly veering to one side. I freaked. Still smiling, Barry quickly took over the controls and righted the plane and got us back on course.

The truth is, Barry was fully in control the entire flight. He's the one who checked the engine before we left the ground. He engineered a great takeoff and would later ease us down for our landing. He got us into a position that was right on course in the middle of open air. He knew exactly what he was doing. He also knew I'd be thrilled to get a taste of flying myself, so he gave me the controls. But even though I was experiencing the thrill of flying, and I suppose I could have jerked the yoke and sent us into a tailspin that even Barry couldn't stop, it was really Barry who was the pilot for that flight. My part was a bit like Bill Murray in the movie *What About Bob,* when he was strapped to the mast of a boat and shouting, "Look, I'm a sailor! I'm a sailor! I sail!"

Once we've genuinely surrendered our lives to Christ, He takes the controls of our lives and begins to navigate a steady path toward His purpose for us. Along the way He loves to see us fly in freedom, so He offers us the controls. But He's still in charge; He's forever and always the King—and we wouldn't want it any other way, because He Himself is really what our epic story is all about.

Your Takeaway

Plot Points

- The call to live an unlimited life is transcended by the call of the cross.
- The King is the central figure in your God-breathed epic life.
- The King's glory and the good of His kingdom are your chief motivations behind your mission as the hero in your life story.
- Your enemy is always trying to direct your focus away from the King.

Dialogue with a Sage

- Why is the cross of Christ at the center of true life? Think of every reason you can.

- What do you understand the kingdom of God to be?
- In what ways would you like to know God better?
- In what ways are you most often tempted to have your focus directed away from God?

From the Script

"For at the right time Christ will be revealed from heaven by the blessed and only almighty God, the King of kings and Lord of lords" (1 Timothy 6:15).

chapter nine

THE SIDEKICK & THE SAGE

Others in Your Story

Destiny usually comes in pairs.

Adam and Eve. Moses and Aaron. David and Jonathan. Paul and Timothy. Antony and Cleopatra. Huckleberry Finn and Tom Sawyer. Sir Edmund Hillary and Tenzing Norgay. Bonnie and Clyde. Batman and Robin.

And Christ and His church.

There's something built deeply into every one of us that longs for the company of another. Something that feels oddly far from home until our soul is genuinely connected with someone else's. Call it romance or friendship or leadership. We were created to be better off when we're with others. Ecclesiastes says it simply: "Two are better than one" (4:9, NIV).

More Alive

Elevenmile Canyon is tucked away neatly into the folds of mountains and valleys that make up the great state of Colorado. It's a God-breathed slice of earth—powerful, pristine, and engagingly beautiful. In places the red canyon walls push upward and leave the rushing river below in a shadow of swirling water. Upstream, the water is milder as it winds gently through a high mountain meadow. The smell of pine mixed with sage is everywhere. From my home in Colorado Springs, it takes exactly one hour and twenty-seven minutes to be standing in the South Platte River, on a particular bend just before the first God-carved tunnel of the canyon. That includes taking the time to rig my fly rod and pull myself into a trusty pair of waders.

Usually, I fish alone. It's how I like it. But one day was different, and on that day I was even more alive. I was with my brother, Luke.

For several years now, Luke and I have made it a tradition to carve out a few days to lose ourselves on the water in search of fish. Actually, we're in search of something much more elusive—we're in search of our souls. Each of us is a pretty good fisherman on his own, but somehow when we're together, trout seem to put up a riverwide alert. To say we generally come up shorthanded would be telling you the truth. And yet, every year as we begin our trip, we talk about the great catch ahead and have a blast setting up the prize for whoever catches the most fish of the day, which usually includes a steak dinner and the next day's flies.

As I stood in the waist-deep water we've dubbed Bolin Hole, I couldn't help it. A smile stretched from ear to ear as I stood waving a rod over my head in almost perfect unison with Luke, who was standing no more than twenty feet away.

He's nearly nine years younger than me; I was off to college when he was still in fifth grade. So while growing up, we never fought with wooden swords together, or joined forces to build a clubhouse out of old pieces of wood, or shared adventures in the field across the street. But over the past few years, the gap in our ages has shrunk to what feels like months. We've become friends. More than that, we've touched a part of each other's soul that only brothers can. We've laughed together, cried together, and fought together.

> We've touched each other's soul as only brothers can.

Now we easily play together—though fishing poles and snowboards have replaced the would-be baseball bats and swords. I can tell you, I'm better when he's with me. The mountain of life seems easier to climb.

Best Friends

Unlike Luke and me, Harrison and Chandler are only a year and a half apart, and without question, they're best friends.

A few days ago, I pulled up to the house after a day of work and was greeted at the front door by two little boys stripped down to their underwear, with brightly colored hobby feathers taped to their foreheads. "Hey, Dad, we're Indians." I started to tell them Indians don't exactly look like that, and we really don't call them Indians anymore. They didn't seem to get my point, and quickly interrupted. "Dad, Grandma brought us your old bow and arrows." And they ran into the living room.

My mother was visiting from Omaha and had brought with her two plastic bows and a fake leather quiver that my dad had given me when I was ten. She figured the boys would love them. She figured right. My boys are only three and four, and the bows were taller than they are. In the middle of the living room was a teepee made of three yardsticks and a couple of bath towels. The boys were jumping up and down, clapping their hands over their mouths and dancing in a circle around the towel teepee. I shook my head and smiled as I wondered where they'd seen it before.

Then the boys took me outside to show me where they'd shot arrows off our back porch. Harrison was proud that he'd shot one over our fence. Sarah was mortified that he might have hit the neighbor's dog, especially after Harrison said he'd been hunting. That's a typical day for Harrison and Chandler. If it isn't bows and arrows, it's kitchen apron–superhero capes and make-believe laser guns. These two guys have found at three and four what it took thirty years for Luke and me to discover...the power of another.

Ecclesiastes was right—two are better than one. And in the epic adventure that is your life, you'll find a few people who help make the journey easier and the mission more secure.

Two of the most significant of these companions are what we can call the sage and the sidekick.

Voice of the Sage

I'll always remember a rock climbing experience I had in the Garden of the Gods in the summer of 1995. I was with my good friend Jim Stack. A graduate of the National Outdoor Leadership School, Jim is a consummate outdoorsman and expert climber.

Even though by then I'd climbed a good bit in my life, serious heights still freaked me out. But I coolly accepted an offer to join Jim in climbing Montezuma's Tower.

As we climbed with Jim in the lead, at one point I was unsure of what to do next.

Then I heard my friend shouting down to me: "Watch me."

I looked up. And the words stuck.

Watch me. That's pretty good advice in life. For help, there's always someone else we can observe. If you want to learn to live beyond your limits, it's wise to take a look at the lives of others who've already done it. And then ask yourself: How did they think? Who did they trust? What did they do?

These people include parents, friends, teachers, and coaches. The corporate world calls such a person a "life coach." I call that person a sage. *Sage* is an old word that means "wise one." Sages are the people who've taught and inspired us to live beyond ourselves. Generally, they're people we have some sort of consistent contact with and who we've put ourselves in a position to learn from.

Then there are sages worth watching that we haven't met personally. I've heard it said, "There is no history, only biography." History is full of the stories of people who have lived unlimited lives in unique and compelling ways. Through the pages of great literature and the verse of song, we can learn timeless lessons of life.

One of the traits of people who make an impact is that they employ a sage or a team of sages to help them get through life more successfully.

Marks of a Sage

In my climb with Jim that day, I got into a rhythm, as you often do when you're climbing. That is, until I hit the crux of the climb. For some reason, I totally froze. It was like my feet couldn't move. My pulse suddenly kicked into overdrive and I could feel my heart pounding through my chest. My legs began to get that rubbery, what-the-heck-am-I-doing-here feeling.

Jim figured out what was happening. Though at this point I couldn't see him above me, the first thing Jim did was paint a picture for me of the rock face I was on. I couldn't believe it. He was out of sight from me and there was no way he could spot exactly where I was climbing. But he'd been where I was, remembered it, and knew exactly what to tell me to do. For the next half hour, Jim skillfully and calmly gave me step-by-step instructions until I made it all the way up.

That's one of the marks of a good sage or mentor—he or she is someone who's been there before you in whatever terrain you're facing in life, and who can therefore advise you where to move.

Jim pressed me to do what I could never do on my own. All good sages do that; they help us break limits we could never have broken on our own. We can do more with a sage than we can alone.

Robert Blaha and Barry Farah have been board members of my organization for several years, but they were my personal sages before they were ever board members. Both of them are successful businessmen, loving husbands, and great dads to their kids. They're perfect sages for a guy like me who's blazing a trail in business with three kids under the age of five. Over the past few years, Robert and Barry have helped me avoid mistakes that could have been incredibly costly for me.

An effective sage is also marked by honesty. The greatest leaps I've ever taken personally have come after one of my mentors has had a gut-level conversation with me.

After preaching my first sermon at New Life Church, my pastor and sage, Ted Haggard, took me to his office and gently but frankly critiqued my speaking. He coached me on how to stand, how to walk, and even how to tell a story. His unabashed honesty about my speaking has over the years been a priceless key to my success in living out my epic.

Probably the most important role of a sage is that of encourager. Moses encouraged Joshua. Paul encouraged

Timothy. And of course, God is the ultimate Sage, and His Word is full of passages to cheer us on, like this: "Have I not commanded you? Be strong and courageous. Do not be terrified; do not be discouraged, for the LORD your God will be with you wherever you go" (Joshua 1:9, NIV).

You may be reading this book with a sage who's helping and encouraging you, and if so, you can attest to the fact that it makes all the difference. Or maybe you've never really had a mentor or a coach, but now you're ready for one. I encourage you to seek out someone who exemplifies the traits and qualities mentioned above.

The Sidekick

For a moment, think of your epic life as a mountain climb. Picture yourself making a steep ascent. You've got a pack on your back, and you're gripping a rope. Picture yourself with both arms stretched out, one above you and one below you, with the rope passing through both your hands.

Attached to that rope is someone following your lead.

You've got two other people with you. Holding on to the rope above you is your sage or mentor, leading the way and encouraging you.

Also attached to that rope is a person below who's following *your* lead, someone you're helping up.

In the parlance of movies and stories, let's think of that person we're helping as the sidekick. Nearly every great hero has a faithful sidekick. Don Quixote had his squire, Sancho. Sherlock Holmes had Dr. Watson. For William Wallace, it was his friend Hamish. In *Raiders of the Lost Ark,* Indiana Jones had Marion. Frodo teamed up with his gardener, Samwise Gamgee. And it was rare to find Han Solo without Chewy.

As important as a good sage is, it's just as important to have at least one person we're helping up the mountain of life. Jesus commanded us to "go and make disciples" (Matthew 28:19). He wasn't talking to just the preachers or full-time ministry people. He was talking to all of us. Part of being successful in your epic life is taking someone with you on the journey. As leadership author John Maxwell often states, there can be no success without a successor.

Some people don't feel qualified or "godly" enough to be a sage to someone else. But helping guide someone else may be the best way to actively deal with and overcome your own insecurities. The Bible says, "A generous man will prosper; he who refreshes others will himself be refreshed" (Proverbs 11:25, NIV). So begin looking and praying about someone you can help.

Such a person shouldn't be hard to find. Everyone is looking for someone to look up to and take life cues from. Often it's just a matter of opening your eyes and seeing their need, and stepping in to help.

And there's one key aspect in which your help for others attains its greatest value.

Soul Connection

"As for me," the prophet Samuel said on one occasion to the people of Israel, "far be it from me that I should sin against the LORD by failing to pray for you. And I will teach you the way that is good and right" (1 Samuel 12:23, NIV). We need to be willing to pay the high price of personal prayer for any-one whom God has entrusted to us.

Prayer always takes a relationship to a different level. I keep a short list of the people God has entrusted to me. I try to know what's happening with each one specifically—

struggles, victories, romances. I pray for them individually, which helps me truly connect with them in my soul.

One of my sages, Terry Felber, often reminds me that he prays for me nearly every day. And he doesn't just say it as a nice Christian thing to say. He means it. About a year ago, Terry moved over one thousand miles away. To know that he continues to pray for me is like continuing to have a guide even when he's not there physically. It means the world.

You've heard the saying that no man is an island. Well, it's just not true. Some have chosen to be islands, and pursue their lives in the isolation of self, refusing to seek counsel or make significant relationships. Tragically, it means missing out on their true destiny. And it's a tragedy that's totally preventable.

If you haven't already, find someone to be a sage in your life, plus someone for whom you can be a sage. You can't help but discover personally just how much you benefit from both, as you continue on your epic climb and reach the destiny that comes only in pairs.

Your Takeaway

Plot Points

- Destiny usually comes in pairs.
- You can do more in a group of two or more than you can alone.
- A sage can be of incomparable assistance in advising you and encouraging you.
- You are also meant to be a helpful sage to others.

Dialogue with a Sage

- Who have been the most influential mentors or sages in your life? Who are the most influential now?
- How have you benefited most from mentors or sages?
- In whose life are you serving now as a sage?
- Do you ever feel tempted to want to be an island, shut off from others? What brings that temptation? What is the best way to respond to it?
- What do you fear most about being accountable to someone?
- What do you fear most about having someone be accountable to you?

From the Script

"The heartfelt counsel of a friend is as sweet as perfume and incense" (Proverbs 27:9).

part**three**

THE

JOURNEY

chapter ten

PASSION

The Hero's Heart for God

Pictures of passion burn deeply into us. Maximus the gladiator brushing his hands through the stalks of wheat in a vision as his wife and son run toward him. Rose reaching out her hand as Jack whispers, "I'll never let go," then falls into the icy ocean while the *Titanic* sinks in the background.

An epic loses its meaning without a passion that transcends the hero. Your epic story and mine are no different.

Forgotten First Love

It was a warm spring night in 1989. I was a freshman at Oral Roberts University in Tulsa. I carefully pedaled my mountain bike around a parking lot behind the towering City of Faith medical complex. I must have looked totally normal, except for the six-pack of beer dangling from my handlebars and the pack of cigarettes tucked in my shirt pocket.

I was feeling glad to be out of the spotlight. *Thank God for out-of-state schools.* For most of my high school years, I'd been in positions of spiritual leadership, constantly under the microscope and watched by everyone. Frankly, I was tired of it. At ORU I thought I could blend in, follow the crowd, and never be noticed.

I was one of those Jesus was talking to when He said, "I hold this against you: You have forsaken your first love" (Revelation 2:4, NIV). I never meant to forsake that love. I never intentionally set out to push God off the center of the canvas. I never planned on my heart growing cool. I never even felt it. Actually, I didn't even suspect it. That's the way it usually happens. It's the worst death of all—slowly, quietly, without your ever knowing. Somewhere along the way I lost my passion for Jesus. But God scripted this late-night bike ride as the setting to begin me on the journey of my lifelong epic.

Throughout history, we've been given fantastic stories of the hunt. The early explorers searched endlessly for gold. Columbus crossed uncharted seas in search for a passage to India. Braving the brutal Arctic and Antarctic oceans, Peary, Amundsen, Scott, and Shackleton sought the undiscovered North and South Poles. The instinct to seek out something bigger than we are is in us. Every epic movie ever made is about it.

So it's no wonder I was looking for something, too. I was searching for a passion that had somehow evaded me. That night, under the moon and stars and the shadow of a towering building, I had a meeting with God. I thought I'd come to this campus to hide and do my own thing. Little did I know I was actually looking for something—my heart and the passion it holds.

I had stopped my bike and walked to a small hill to relish in my so-called freedom. Before I could even enjoy the moment, it hit me. I suddenly realized the cans and smokes I was carrying represented an intentional hike away from

God. My heart suddenly rushed out of me. It was starving. It wasn't sin or secrets or solitude I craved. It was God. My story had taken a wrong turn and tonight God wanted to straighten out the plot. It hit me like a ton of bricks. I felt like the psalmist when he said, "I seek you with all my heart; do not let me stray from your commands" (Psalm 119:10, NIV). Suddenly, everything inside of me desperately and deeply wanted God. I remember thinking to myself, *Where on earth has this feeling been?*

> It was an intentional hike away from God.

I tossed the beer and cigarettes into the trash and dashed across the parking lot. I crawled under the chain-link fence of the baseball stadium and made my way up the cement steps. In the dead of night, I found my seat somewhere in left field (that location seemed appropriate—and it would become my hiding place during the rest of my time at ORU). For the next few hours, I sat and thought, then cried, then prayed, then prayed and cried some more. This was real. I wanted it. I wanted more of Him. I remembered the passion and life and love and fire of God I'd known, and I was determined to get it back.

I should have known it would return. What I didn't realize that night was that though I was seeking after passion, passion was equally seeking after me. I was, as C. S. Lewis said, the mouse chasing the cat. In our absurdity of thinking we can catch God, He turns on us and runs straight into us. I rediscovered the core of the 252 Matrix and the secret of the unlimited life.

Pleasing God

Luke 2:52 tells us that Jesus grew "in favor with God" (NIV). You'd think that Jesus wouldn't have to grow in favor with

God; after all, He was God's very Son in the flesh. I think God is making an emphatic point in that passage, one that's reflected also at a later time, when Jesus came up out of the water after being baptized in the Jordan: "And a voice from heaven said, "This is my beloved Son, and I am fully pleased with him"" (Matthew 3:17).

Pleasing God—growing in favor with Him—is central to everything else in our lives. It's the motivation and meaning of our story.

God wants us to understand that life without Him is absolutely meaningless. Every day, thousands of people accomplish thousands of self-imposed goals and still feel empty at the end of it all. Why? Because life isn't about us. Before we were ever born, God designed us exactly as we are with *His purpose* in mind for us. Only when we recognize this at our spiritual core, and get our hearts in line with His heart, can we accomplish anything of genuine significance.

The Bible says, "It's in Christ that we find out who we are and what we are living for. Long before we first heard of Christ and got our hopes up, he had his eye on us, had designs on us for glorious living, part of the overall purpose he is working out in everything and everyone" (Ephesians 1:11–12, *The Message*). Think of that! Unless we grow in relationship with God, our personal aspirations and attempts at a meaningful life are hopeless.

That night, in the middle of left field, I asked myself some pretty tough questions. For a moment, I was totally naked with God. And it didn't matter. I knew I could be myself. Broken, humbled, and vulnerable. I remembered that "neither height nor depth, nor anything else in all creation, will be able to separate us from the love of God that is in Christ Jesus our Lord" (Romans 8:39, NIV). Nothing. No sin. No secret. Nothing. I held on to that promise that night. God did the rest.

Imagine, for a moment, your own seat in an otherwise empty stadium. Maybe you've walked with God all your life, or maybe you've never experienced God's rushing love. Can I dare you to take off your shell of self for a moment? If you were to level with yourself, where would you say you are on your faith journey?

When was the last time you cried in the presence of God?

Do you know what really pleases God?

Do you find yourself sharing your faith in God with those around you?

Is God's Word alive in you…or is it a chore to read the Bible?

Do you feel like your life is a result of your own effort or God's mission?

God Waits for You

If your answers to these questions lead you to believe that you need a God-moment, go and have one. Really. Right now, tonight, this weekend—as soon as you can. Find a mountain or a closet or a stadium seat and get to business with God. Maybe you need a bit of searching, as I did. Remember, if you'll look for Him, He'll always be found. After all, He's searching for you, too.

When Sarah and I were in college together, our dorm buildings were attached by a common room we called the Fishbowl. On Friday nights, the Fishbowl would fill up with guys and girls waiting for their dates to come down the elevator of the opposite building. I remember countless Fridays I spent there, waiting in the lobby. My heart would be racing, my palms sweating, and my head spinning. I was whipped. No question about it. The minutes would chug by like hours as I waited. And when she finally made her grand entrance, it was like seeing her for the first time, every time. Know the feeling? That's exactly how God waits for you. He longs to spend time with you, to get to know you, to rush over you all over again. And that's the core of unlimited passion and the heart of the hero.

Without trust in God and a strong conviction about developing your spiritual sphere, it's virtually impossible to live a balanced and effective life. Some would say there are a lot of ways to achieve spiritual centeredness—Zen meditation, yoga, even positive self-talk. In reality, there's only one way to fill the spiritual dimension of life, and that's through Jesus Christ. There's something about a relationship with Jesus that makes life passionately fulfilling.

So many people spend their lives only killing time. And the enemy loves it. Life without God, without passion, is either empty or meaninglessly busy. But Jesus came to Planet Earth to pay the ultimate price so we could experience what H. G. Wells and Byron and Barton only dreamed of—a deep well that gives life meaning.

Unless we first deal with this core issue of spiritual passion, our life's story loses its meaning. But in discovering the fullness of abiding in Christ, all of life becomes a full horizon of purpose. Imagine your deepest, most intimate moment with the Savior. Now imagine there's an even greater experience with Him. That's limitless passion.

Encounter with Passion

Passion calls to all of us. Our heart longs to be freely connected with God—and His heart longs to be freely connected with ours. You've probably felt Him calling. It may have happened through the voice of an evangelist or a pastor or a teacher. Or maybe it came in the way the sun paints a brilliant canvas over the sky for a few moments on a summer night. Maybe in the sound of a baby's laugh or the silence of a moonlit morning. Moments that catch our breath and engulf our hearts. Could that really be God? C. S. Lewis groped for the best word to describe it—*joy* was the closest he could come. John Eldredge and Brent Curtis called it "the sacred romance."

Some twenty centuries ago, two friends walked down a road one afternoon toward a village called Emmaus. On the way, they were joined by a stranger. After a long and very engaging talk along the journey, the two friends reached their destination. It was nearly evening, so they invited the stranger to stay with them for the night. Moments later, as they sat down together for a meal and He broke bread and gave thanks, the two men suddenly realized that this stranger was actually the resurrected Christ. That same moment, He disappeared.

> Passion was calling to us, wasn't it?

Immediately they asked each other, "Were not our hearts burning within us while he talked with us on the road and opened the Scriptures to us?" (Luke 24:32, NIV). They might just as well have said, "On the road, *passion* was calling to us, wasn't it? Did you feel it?"

Chances are, Jesus has been with you and you didn't even know it. Your heart was burning, but you may have shrugged it off as just a "nice" moment. Think about it. The feeling after a touching movie or a certain song or a particular smell. "Hey, wait a minute, I *did* feel something."

Passion is looking for you. The Bible tells us that Jesus came alongside the two disciples on the Emmaus road; He drew near, then started walking with them. *They* didn't join *Him;* He joined them. They were already in midconversation when the very subject of that conversation walked up in person and joined in. He probed to get them to talk about their feelings for Him. Jesus loves to watch us pursue Him, even as He seeks us out.

As these two friends approached Emmaus, the Bible tells us that Jesus "acted as if he were going farther" (Luke 24:28, NIV). He didn't really intend to leave them yet, though it looked as if He did. Actually, I think He wanted to hear them ask Him to stay; He wanted to hear them express their longing for His presence, though their conscious minds at this point didn't comprehend who He was. They did ask; and of course He agreed. And they soon discovered who He really was.

Everything

Even now, another hero walks a dusty road on the first leg of his journey, perhaps unsure if it's even the right road. It might be you. Are you walking along life's road, kicking up dust, wondering where God is? Are you desperate over the loss of a job or a friend or a dream? Are you scared that life is passing you by?

Look over your shoulder. Chances are, you'll see a Man coming alongside to walk with you. Take a moment and talk to Him. See the gleam in His eye? That's passion calling.

Steven Covey is right: "We aren't human beings having a spiritual experience; we're spiritual beings having a human experience." We are, at our core, spiritual. There's something in every one of us that longs to connect with something more deeply spiritual than we are—passion. That's God crying out for us to seek after Him.

One of our modern worship songs says it so well: He's the air we breathe, and our daily bread, and without Him we're desperate and lost.

God isn't interested in being a part of our lives. He wants to be all of our lives. He wants to be the air we breathe, the songs we sing, the work we do, the play we enjoy, the very essence of our being. He wants to be everything in us.

Actually, He wants our lives to be exchanged for His. That's what the crucified life is all about. Exchanging our lives for His. Dying daily to our own petty sins and vanities and leadings, and calling out to Him in desperate whole-life worship. Not just part of us, but everything. Body, mind, soul, and spirit. Every part, crying out for more of who He is, hungry and thirsty for more of Him.

Life, after all, really is all about Him. He alone brings meaning and order and a sense of why to all of it. To attempt to accomplish or achieve or break limits, either personal or otherwise, without Him, would be like trying to make coffee without coffee beans. God isn't a part of life; He *is* life. He isn't a piece of the puzzle; He's the complete picture we're trying to put together. God is at the very core of the very core of existence. It's impossible to separate the idea of limitless living from Him.

Turbocharged by Love

The 252 Matrix gives us a picture of a growing, forward-moving life. At the very core of that life is passion for Jesus. Without it, the other areas of 252 are vanity. With it, they're turbocharged for an incredible journey.

Think about it again: Jesus grew in favor with God. The relationship between the Father in heaven and the Son in human form expanded, strengthened, and deepened during those eighteen years of maturing. It blows my mind. But that's the nature of God. It's deeper and further than we could ever possibly imagine.

Now get this: In John 15:9 we read, "I have loved you even as the Father has loved me." That's Jesus talking…to *us!* Do we know how much the Father loves Jesus? We think we have a good idea about it—God must love Jesus infinitely, endlessly, boundlessly. "Well," Jesus is saying, "that's how much I love you! That's how incredibly much I want to expand your life and passion and experience with Me."

One of the first steps in passionately loving God is realizing that He passionately loves us first. He's the One who tells us, "Before you loved Me, I have loved you. Before you searched for Me, I was searching for you."

I love the song "His Love Is Loud." It says it all. God's love for you and for me is so loud, it echoes though hell and bounces off eternity. It screams in the majesty of the mountains. It thunders in the mist of an ocean's breaking surf. And when Passion was nailed to a tree, His love roared as the skies crashed and lightning flashed.

> That's how much I want to expand your life.

Jesus' Passion

No one in world history has demonstrated more passion in a more powerful way than Jesus. Romance novels, war movies, and professional sports coaches attempt to capture passion, but all of them seem to fall short somehow.

Mel Gibson, the director and star of *Braveheart*, one of the most daring and moving films of the past decade, understands the power of God's passion. He's just finished filming what he considers to be the most important film of his life. Its title is *The Passion*. It portrays the final hours of Jesus' life on earth, leading up to His crucifixion and resurrection. Step aside, William Wallace.

"Greater love has no one than this," Jesus said, "that one lay down his life for his friends" (John 15:13, NIV). And no one has ever done that in the way Jesus did. The living God willingly gave us His one and only Son to be brutally killed in exchange for our lives. Now that's passion. Harlequin doesn't have a thing on the story of the cross. *Gladiator* is wimpy compared to the power of Good Friday.

The epic of the cross is the most powerful story in all of human history. Never before had anyone done so much for so many, and never again would that passion be matched. The very idea of unlimited living begins and ends at Calvary. Jesus didn't settle for an average life or an average ministry. And He certainly didn't settle for an average death—not to mention the uniqueness of His resurrection and ascension.

In the same way, your own journey beyond average begins with a hero's heart—your passion for God. With it, you're driven by something greater than yourself. Without it, you're driven only by your own will, which is certain to fade or fail along the course.

Either way, God calls to you and me. Passion is waiting to set your heart on fire. You'll need it to see the way.

Your Takeaway

Plot Points

- Our hearts long to be fully connected with God's heart.
- Unless we take care of our spiritual core, our journey will feel empty.
- Like the men on the road to Emmaus, Jesus wants to hear us invite Him to be part of our story.

Dialogue with a Sage

- How would you describe passion for God? What does it look like?

- Who are the people you know who are most passionate for God? How do you sense this passion in them?
- What kind of passionate encounter with God do you long for?
- What is it that most often stands in the way of your being passionate for God?
- What do you need to do to maintain consistent passion for God?

From the Script

"He died for everyone so that those who receive his new life will no longer live to please themselves. Instead, they will live to please Christ, who died and was raised for them" (2 Corinthians 5:15).

chapter eleven

STRATEGY

The Hero's Mind

Your passionate heart will lead you to the right path...and a renewed mind will help you navigate it.

When I was a youth pastor, I must have seen *The Princess Bride*—one of the few safe films for youth groups—a hundred times. One of my favorite scenes from the movie is the battle of wits between the short Sicilian, Vizzini, and the story's hero—the man in black.

You remember the scene: On a table between them are two goblets of wine, one of them poisoned. After the goblets are scrambled, they'll each choose one to drink from. They banter at length about the strategy involved, then the choice is made. Vizzini is sure he's won; he berates the hero for forgetting a "classic" rule: "Never go against a Sicilian when death is on the line." He cackles in uncontrolled laughter—then abruptly falls over dead. Death was on the line...but he lost the battle of the mind.

That reminds me of one of my own near brushes with death.

Battle Strategy

This shouldn't be happening to me, I thought as I rechecked the trigger of the gun I was holding. My hand had stopped bleeding for the moment and I quickly wrapped it with a piece of my shredded T-shirt. A bullet whizzed by my head. Instinctively, I dropped to the ground a few yards from a large rock.

My heart was pounding and my shirt was soaked in sweat. I desperately needed a place to hide. Somewhere off in the distance, I heard a voice. "John, to your right! To your right!" Another bullet. Without thinking, I lunged toward the boulder. My hands were shaking uncontrollably and I wondered if I'd even have what it takes to pull the trigger if I needed to. Shots rang out all around me. I could feel my heart beating. *Why did I come out to the woods today? What in the world was I thinking?*

I inched toward a row of trees that led into deeper forest. The pounding of bullets seemed to quiet for a moment. I tried to slow my breathing. I carefully glanced out around the corner of the rock. No one. Nothing except dirt and rocks. I made my move. And then it began.

First from behind. "Blam!" The first bullet hit my left leg and I fell back to the ground with a thud. A cold sting ripped through my body. Then I saw them. No more than ten feet away were two men with guns pointed directly at me. I dropped my weapon and tried to cover my head, but it was no use. Like a rainstorm of fire, bullets pelted my arms, legs, and back. I just wanted to get out alive.

As quickly as it had begun, it was over. Unbelievably, I was still breathing. I heard a voice somewhere behind me: "Another game? Or are you gonna let a couple of interns whip you?"

Paintball has forever been a nemesis for me. For some reason, every time I play, my team loses miserably. I think it has something to do with strategy. Our staff team was in better shape and had more collective life experience than our lowly interns, who had challenged us to a few games of paintball. But the one thing our intern counterparts had that we didn't was strategy—carefully planned and patiently carried out. They used their collective heads wisely. And because we didn't, we couldn't win despite our advantages. In effect, our lack of brainpower became our greatest barrier to winning.

And so it can be for you, our hero. Passion is central for success in completing your mission, but unless you're also armed with wisdom, you're almost certain to make mistakes along the way. In a society that moves at an eye-popping pace where fast is the measure of success, mental fitness isn't a luxury; it's a necessity. People who fail to shape their minds will have their minds shaped by others. As author and pastor Gordon MacDonald writes in *Ordering Your Private World,* "They are victimized because they have not taught themselves to think; nor have they set themselves to the lifelong pursuit of the growth of the mind. Not having the facility of a strong mind, they grow dependent upon the thoughts and opinions of others. Rather than deal with ideas and issues, they reduce themselves to lives full of rules, regulations, and programs."

Change your mind and unlock your future.

Bottom line: Change your mind and unlock your future. Ignore your mind and take a gamble with your life.

Thought is the castle in the kingdom of the mind where knowledge is queen and wisdom is king. Knowledge relies on information to process thought, whereas wisdom pulls on the strength of life experience and the ability to reason to an appropriate end. The full life Jesus modeled for us in the 252 Matrix offers more than a boundless relationship with God, total health, and deeply meaningful relationships. It also includes the possibility of living without a cap on your mind—a life of unlimited wisdom.

Mind Muscle

Millions of people in Iraq rejoiced after the fall of Saddam Hussein, the dictator who had stolen their freedom, their futures, and their freedom to think. As one Muslim cleric there declared after seeing Saddam's statue toppled in the center of Baghdad, "I have never lived a single day...now I can start living."

The Iraqis are recapturing their freedom to think. But are we losing ours? In today's world, we're so easily convinced or controlled into not thinking for ourselves. Unfortunately, it happens every day in every part of the world. Sometimes people are fooled in blatant ways, but more often it's much subtler. We're amazed at how a cult leader like Jim Jones or David Koresh can convince vulnerable people that he can do their thinking for them. But MTV, network news, and myriad commercials vie for our brains and decisions every day. I think I bought a six-pack of Mountain Dew the other day just because I'd seen a great ad during a football game.

It's easier to let someone else think for us than it is to think for ourselves. That's the pattern of the world. But Paul tells us, "Don't copy the behavior and customs of this world, but let God transform you into a new person by changing the way you think" (Romans 12:2). We can either allow the world around us to dictate our thoughts, or we can learn to think for ourselves, being influenced and led by the Spirit and Word of God.

The mind is like a muscle. To work properly, it must be used and exercised. God designed you with a brain that's one of the most intricate and fantastic devices the world has ever known. Fully engaging in life means fully engaging the mind He's given us. "One of the saddest experiences which can come to a human being," V. W. Burrows said, "is to awaken, gray-haired and wrinkled, near the close of an unproductive career, to the fact that all through the years he has been using only a small part of himself." Don't waste your life by wasting your mind. Determine to fully engage your brain and get all you can out of what God has given you. He created our world full of mysteries for us to uncover and discover.

God's Thoughts

A few years ago, I realized I'd nearly stopped learning. I would read or study just enough to get by. If I was preparing a talk, I'd dig up a few old books and flip through my Bible, but I wasn't exercising my brain. I was in danger of becoming like too many people who allow their brains to atrophy, embracing only amusement (which, incidentally, literally means the absence of thought) and ignoring good thinking. A big part of life is having fun, but truthfully, using our minds can be a blast. My wife, Sarah, has always been a voracious reader, sometimes reading two or three books a week. She especially loves biographies. Now, as often as possible, we read together. Not the same books, but at the same time. I know she's mining gold from her books and I love to sit and discuss what we're learning. Where once my brain was starting to run on fumes, I've begun filling it again. I can tell you, it has made all the difference in my writing, speaking, and overall ability to communicate. Undoubtedly, I have more to give.

We ought to glorify God with our minds by contributing to others with new ideas, inventions, and information. We ought to be the ones who establish institutions that live on long after we're gone. We shouldn't be content to sit on the sidelines as others develop concepts for government, economics, and science. We need to be determined to worship God with all our minds by allowing Him to inspire us to create art and write good literature. After all, where do wisdom and good ideas originate?

God is the source of all true wisdom and life strategy. "The fear of the LORD is the beginning of wisdom" (Psalm 111:10, NIV), and that fear includes reverence and wonder and awe. How many of us limit the ideas God has for us simply because we fail to look upward to Him in wonder and fear when it comes to developing our mind? Think about it. God is the ultimate source of wisdom and knowledge. He holds in His hand the most complex formulas of the universe. He fully understands the black holes and ocean depths and DNA strands that we can only begin to comprehend. To Him, our most complex theories are simple. Our breakthroughs in genetics and science and technology are millions of millennia behind Him. How can we be more interested in looking to ourselves for strategy than to Him?

Looking inward is perfectly natural as human beings. Pop culture and modern humanism tells us to look to ourselves for the answers. Philosophy often teaches us that wisdom is totally relative and self-regulated, and we often attempt to recreate wisdom and meaning in "our own image." But that's as impossible as gravity reversing itself. As Job said, "True wisdom and power are with God; counsel and understanding are his" (Job 12:13). God is the source of life's limit-breaking ideas. He's the architect you can fully trust with your mind.

> A heart submitted to God will lead to a mind submitted to God.

So how do we learn God's thoughts?

Paul tells us, "No one can know God's thoughts except

God's own Spirit" (1 Corinthians 2:11). The first step toward strategic living is developing the spiritual sphere of the 252 Matrix by fully embracing Spirit-filled living and pursuing passion. Paul goes on to say that if we've truly submitted our lives to God, then "we have the mind of Christ" (2:16). So if we've crucified our old self and taken on a Spirit-breathed life, we have access to God's wisdom, His plans, His ideas. A heart submitted to God will lead to a mind submitted to God, which leads to a life submitted to God.

Seeing Reality

By intentionally renewing our minds, it becomes much more difficult for the enemy to pry his way into our lives and deceive us into believing limiting thoughts, which lead to limiting actions and, ultimately, limited lives.

One of the central themes in the movie *The Matrix* was the idea that the reality we accept is often not reality at all. To people who were living in it, the illusion of the Matrix had become so real that they failed to question it at all.

The villain of our lives is the father of lies, and he loves to persuade us that what's true is false and what's false is true. We've got to beat him at his own game. The best way to get your mind in shape is to use it. Ask questions. Actually study the Word of God. Read some of the countless good books that are out there and available on every subject imaginable. Challenge yourself to think outside the box. Stretch your mind, shape it, fill it with truth. Whatever you do, don't waste it. Remember, your mind doesn't belong to you, but to God; you're stewarding *His* mind, not yours.

Jesus tells us to love the Lord our God with all our mind—not just part of our mental capacity, but all of it. We love and honor Him by the way we steward the gift of wisdom God offers to all of us. And the best way to steward the gift of wisdom is to develop it, nurture it, and get more of it.

Get Wisdom

There are a lot of things I can't do simply because I've never been taught how to do them. I can't build my own computer. I can't control a sailboat. I can't change the carburetor in my Honda Accord. I can't pilot an airplane. Why? Is it because I don't want to? Not necessarily. Is it because I'm not interested? I'd love to know how to do those things. Why then?

Simple: I haven't learned how. Often the difference between living beyond the limits and living blockaded is nothing more than information. One of the greatest limitations in life is simply a lack of knowledge. Seems plain enough, and yet so many of us fail to expand this part of us.

For some reason, the idea of developing our brains for Christ is sometimes interpreted as self-reliance, a waste of time, and not as "pure" as lots of other pursuits. Big mistake. I've met too many young career people who passionately love God but who failed to develop their ability to think strategically or to gather information. They often find themselves at a severe disadvantage and wind up resorting to careers and endeavors that require less aptitude or knowledge. Usually they make excuses for why they haven't done the things they felt God wanted them to do. They wander through life blaming others for their own lack of discipline to do what Solomon encouraged his sons to do over and over and over: *Get wisdom!*

Jesus said, "Much is required from those to whom much is given, and much more is required from those to whom much more is given" (Luke 12:48). As a generation that has been given much—much information, access to great thinkers and big ideas—we're responsible to steward what we have. We have more opportunity, more technology, and more education than ever before in the history of the world. Anything less than full-throttle use of our minds would be tragic. Let's be the ones who challenge ourselves to learn more and expand our skills so we can impact more for His kingdom.

God tells us, "Make the most of every opportunity for doing good in these evil days" (Ephesians 5:16)—so let's determine to be always for exactly that. We tend to think some people are just luckier than others when really their success happens simply because they stay prepared for opportunity. Daniel was rewarded for the knowledge he'd gained prior to his big break. Joseph helped a nation out of economic struggle because he had the mental aptitude combined with divine favor. Did God use their mental training? You bet.

Keep in mind that the purpose of stewarding our minds is to influence more people for the kingdom of God, not to expand our own kingdom. Ivy League educations and high-exposure careers aren't necessarily what pleases God. In one story Jesus told, the hero was a beggar named Lazarus (Luke 16:19–20). Another hero He called attention to was an impoverished widow who put her last two coins in the temple treasury (Luke 21:2–4). Another hero was the disciple Dorcas, who performed many deeds of kindness (Acts 9:36–42). Did God use all these people? Of course.

Jerusalem's leaders "were amazed when they saw the boldness of Peter and John, for they could see that they were ordinary men who had had no special training" (Acts 4:13). Ordinary fishermen without exceptional education, but God used them.

Remember, God's Word says, "Has not God chosen those

who are poor in the eyes of the world to be rich in faith and to inherit the kingdom he promised those who love him?" (James 2:5, NIV). Stewardship isn't about what we have, but what we *do* with what we have. And if we've been given opportunity—including educational opportunities—we should be motivated to make the most of it.

For decades, Christianity has been relegated to being a subculture. Let's break out of the limits we've imposed on ourselves and not be satisfied with being a subculture, or even a counterculture, for that matter. Let's be the generation who will have the guts to gain the skills and knowledge to influence every area of culture. Let's break the molds of earlier generations and determine to create godly culture. We can and should influence the fields of entertainment, law, medicine, education, business, politics, and more. We need to learn to be in the world but not of it. God didn't create His church to be anything less than everything it has the potential of becoming. He created us to be Him with skin on. That's a pretty tall order. It means we don't have the luxury of taking the easy road.

> Let's have the guts to gain the skills and knowledge to influence every area of culture.

Ten Times Better

In his book *Good to Great,* Jim Collins points over and over to the value of constant learning, measuring, and evaluating for taking good companies and making them great. That's wisdom at work. And that's exactly what God wants to do—take us from good to great. He isn't looking for average, He's looking for excellence. Of course, it won't be easy. But the hero always anticipates difficulties. David once said, "I cannot present burnt offerings to the LORD my God that have cost me nothing" (2 Samuel 24:24). What will it cost us to offer ourselves to God? It will cost our time, our energy, and our attention, for starters.

He deserves nothing less from us. Let's live "not as unwise but as wise" (Ephesians 5:15, NIV). The watching world will embrace a relevant church far faster than an out-of-touch or ignorant one. The Old Testament tells us that the king of Babylon found the advice from the young Hebrew men Daniel, Shadrach, Meshach, and Abednego "to be ten times better than that of all the magicians and enchanters in his entire kingdom" (Daniel 1:20). Careful attention to their minds led them to influential positions in the kingdom and more glory for God. And that's the point.

God wants us on the cutting edge, not on the back burner. But that's usually where we go when we feel ineffective. Throughout the Old Testament, the Hebrews found themselves in a cycle of obedience, distraction, disobedience, and judgment. When they were in disobedience and God allowed their enemies to oppress them, they would often head for the hills and hide in the caves. How embarrassing! That's not where God intended for them to live. Over and over, God called them back into the land He'd given them. Let's not stay in the caves of our Christian subculture. God is calling us out of the dark dampness of our own little worlds, back into the world that He promised to His Son when He told Him, "I will give you the nations as your inheritance, the ends of the earth as your possession" (Psalm 2:8). You know you've got the nation when you're shaping culture rather than being shaped by it.

Remember, our lives are not our own. Just as Jesus performed miracles in the New Testament to give glory to the Father, we're called to live lives that glorify the King of kings. That means the work we do is a direct reflection on the God we serve. We should do whatever it takes to achieve excellence in everything we do: learn more, read more, and become more of what He wants you to be. Live in such a way that you break the limits that hold you back. Strategic limits will only keep you fenced in; seeking after knowledge and wisdom will lead to strategic freedom.

Free to Think

What do you want to be true about your education and mental training? That it was only mediocre? Or that like Daniel and his friends, God gave you "an unusual aptitude for learning the literature and science of the time"? (Daniel 1:17).

What do you want to be true about how well you understand your faith, and how strongly you testify to it? Will you settle for weakness in this area? Or will you be like Paul, "proclaiming the Kingdom of God with all boldness and teaching about the Lord Jesus Christ"? (Acts 28:31).

What do you want to be true about how you depend on God's help to plan out your life? Will this be only hit-and-miss, or will you constantly experience the truth of Proverbs 16:3—"Commit your work to the LORD, and then your plans will succeed"?

What do you want to be true about your skills and talents? That they were never developed, or that what you do and create and accomplish is "the work of a skilled craftsman"? (Exodus 28:6, NIV).

Where does knowledge come from? Without question, God is the source of all knowledge. He encourages us to read the Word as a way to get understanding. The psalmist cried out to God, "I believe in your commands; now teach me good judgment and knowledge" (Psalm 119:66). Will that be your plea as well?

We also have access to books and other ways of increasing our base of knowledge and skills. As a writer, I've often heard it said that you write what you read. It's true in life, too. You are what you read. We have a terrific legacy of incredible Christian writers to draw from. Take time to get to know C. S. Lewis, George MacDonald, Os Guinness, Philip Yancey, Dallas Willard, and scores of other outstanding authors.

Whatever you do, determine to exercise your brain. After all, you're free—free to chose, free to question, free to think.

And chances are, sooner or later you, too, will be challenged to a battle of wits.

Your Takeaway

Plot Points

- People who fail to shape their minds will have their minds shaped by others.
- Developing your mind increases your future potential and pushes limits.
- For your mind to work properly, it must be exercised.
- Mere amusement atrophies your mind, while reading activates your mind.
- Your mind is changed and renewed through the Word of God.
- God is the source of all true wisdom and life strategy.

Dialogue with a Sage

- How does God want your mind to be renewed?
- What habits have you established to strengthen your mind?

- How can you develop your intellect without sacrificing spiritual truth?
- What books have influenced you most?
- How do you read and study the Bible?
- What other books are you reading?

From the Script

"Let God transform you into a new person by changing the way you think" (Romans 12:2).

chapter twelve

STATURE

The Hero's Strength

It was over. Or at least, that's what it seemed. Neo lay dead on the ground. The Karate Kid lay weak in the training room. Rocky stumbled and slumped against the ropes. The fires of Mordor pressed in around Frodo. The hero has been pushed beyond his most daring dreams. Every ounce of strength seemed to have left him.

The future of the epic pivots on this moment. All is lost, it seems. The villain grins.

Then it happens. It begins like a slow burn. Deep inside the hero, he finds new strength. The music swells, and the hero stands to his feet.

In our hearts, we too want to rise up in this moment—when the tide suddenly changes and the battle is won.

Total Health

For five years Sarah and I tried to have children. Unless you've experienced the pain of childlessness yourself, it's very difficult to understand. For half a decade Sarah and I walked down that dark and lonely path. The pain of not conceiving is fiercely coupled with the agony of trying and waiting and crying, month after endless month. Not unlike the death of a child, it's the loss of "what could be" over and over and over again.

I'll never fully understand the pain Sarah went through during those difficult years. I nursed my own hurt, but I know it only dimly compares to the ache she endured almost daily. Friends tried their best to comfort us, our pastors faithfully prayed for us, and our parents constantly encouraged us. But the ache remained.

Finally, on the counsel of our good friends Michael and Karen Broome, we turned to adoption and even considered in vitro fertilization (IVF). The problems with IVF were complex and the procedure very expensive, but we began the process. Within a few weeks, we received a call that Sarah had been accepted to be part of a test program and our IVF fees would be waived. We were thrilled. As part of the preparation for the procedure, Sarah was admitted for a laparoscopy surgery. Within weeks of that surgery, Sarah was pregnant, without IVF. Apparently, removing the endometriosis jump-started her system.

Nine months later, Harrison Christian was born. It would be impossible to find the right words to express the wild joy I felt the first time I held my little boy. I was more alive that day than I'd ever been. And Sarah was beaming. Our little family had begun so well with this perfect little boy.

We were anxious to bring Harrison home from the hospital to introduce him to his new world of tiny blue jumpers and musical mobiles and embroidered pillows. He'd been five years in the making, and we were ready for him.

So you can imagine how knocked back we were when

the doctor told us Harrison had a high bilirubin count (something relatively common in Colorado's high altitude), and that although we could take him home, he would have to spend a few weeks in a "bili box," a specially designed treatment bed. And we would be able to hold him for only moments at a time.

The thought of bringing home a sick baby was heartbreaking. It was agony. Our precious little boy, the one we'd cried and prayed and hoped for, was desperately out of our reach. By doctor's orders, he was confined to a small bed in what amounted to a clear "suitcase" with a kind of blacklight continually shining on him. We were told he had to be constantly monitored. Sarah and I and her mother established three-hour shifts to keep an eye on him throughout the night.

I still remember watching my darling wife weeping in the middle of the night, as she held the tiny hand of our new baby, her face lit by the eerie blue light of Harrison's bed. I also remember praying throughout the nights for my little man. I remember praying for strength and health and calling. The abundance of bilirubin in his body caused him to be almost totally lethargic.

I asked God to help him grow up strong and full of life.

The energy was zapped right out of him. He struggled to eat and barely moved. I remember asking God to touch his little body and help him grow up tall and strong and full of life. I knew this was God's way, and I wanted it for Harrison.

Harrison is four now and as active and full of energy as any other boy I've ever seen. He loves to run and jump and explore. He's got his daddy's neverending curiosity and his mother's good looks. Even as he grows, I pray the same prayers and have the same hopes for him that I did when he was lying in the suitcase, barely moving. And I think God does the same for us. My heart's desire for Harrison is that he's able to enjoy life as fully as possible. God's desire for us is that we experience the total fullness of the life He's given us—that's total health and the hero's strength.

Luke 2:52 tells us that Jesus grew in stature (NIV). The word *stature* comes from the Latin *statura,* which means "to stand upright." Its root meaning implies good posture, health, and overall physical fitness. Why did Luke include "stature" in his description of how Jesus grew? Probably for the same reason Jesus later told us to love the Lord our God "with all your *strength*" (Mark 12:30, NIV). Stewardship of our physical bodies—specifically our strength and energy—is a vital part of living fully engaged lives for the King.

God's Body

Nearly every epic hero relies to some degree on his inner and outer strength to help him accomplish his mission. The gladiator Maximus used his strength to fight his way to Rome. Without strength, Rocky Balboa wouldn't have become an American legend. And it was both inner and outer strength that Luke Skywalker used against the evil Empire. Each of these heroes understood that strength must be cultivated. Maximus relentlessly practiced before he entered the Colosseum. We all remember Rocky training to meet Apollo Creed, and Luke Skywalker training with Yoda.

Love God "with *all* your strength," Jesus said. So the more strength and energy we have, the more we're able to worship God with it. Repeatedly, God told Joshua to be "strong and courageous" (Joshua 1:9). He was referring to inner strength, but the same Hebrew word for "strong" was also used when describing the physical characteristics of Joshua's fighting men. Paul said "physical exercise has some value, but spiritual exercise is much more important" (1 Timothy 4:8). He wasn't saying physical strength isn't important; it's just not *as* important as spiritual strength.

Our bodies are one of the weapons we've been given to help us fulfill God's epic mission. You might ask, "Isn't it really vanity and arrogance to focus on our bodies so much? Shouldn't we be content just to spend time with God and let Him take care of the rest?" But that's the wrong way to look at it. If we've truly been crucified with Him, our bodies are really not ours at all, but His. Soldiers in the U.S. military are required to take care of their bodies because they're the property of the U.S. government. My cousin J. P., who serves in the army, told me that a soldier isn't allowed to give blood at a public hospital because even his blood belongs to the military!

How much more this is true for us—that our bodies belong to God. So Paul says, "I plead with you to give your bodies to God. Let them be a living and holy sacrifice—the kind he will accept. When you think of what he has done for you, is this too much to ask?" (Romans 12:1). How we treat our bodies, what we put into them, and how we maintain them is much more a worship issue than a fitness issue.

Too many of us are passionate about prayer and church and other religious things, but totally neglect the bodies God gave us as the primary instrument of our worship and service. What good does it do to have a powerful gift of evangelism, or how effective will you be at serving others, if you're constantly sick or exhausted? Poor personal health habits are one of the greatest threats against full-throttle lives.

Strength of the Savior

The fullest meaning of the word *Savior* brings before us the One who makes people healthy and whole. And that's precisely what Jesus came to the world to do—to bring us fully into God's kingdom, where we're totally restored from half living to wholeness in every way: in our emotions, our spirits, our relationships, and our bodies. And Jesus was the perfect example of healthy living. The Bible tells us that Jesus was a carpenter (Mark 6:3)—physically demanding work, even in ancient Israel. Later, in His years of ministry, Jesus must have taken care to maintain His physical strength as He kept up a rigorous travel schedule. It wasn't uncommon for Him to travel twenty miles in a day, preaching and teaching as He went.

We all know the importance of a healthy diet and exercise. And yet so many of us still struggle. Obesity is increasingly common, not only in an overwhelming

> The Savior makes people healthy and whole.

number of adults, but in children as well. We've got to get a handle on it. If we don't, it could single-handedly destroy God's hopes for a generation of potential leaders. In our American culture, we've grown too accustomed to fast food, convenience, and inactivity. In our effort to make life simpler, we've complicated the very mechanism we have to walk through it with—our bodies. Is that the way to worship the King of kings?

A couple of years ago, I found myself constantly tired and out of energy. It was becoming more and more difficult to maintain my usual upbeat persona, and I relied on coffee to give me the boost I needed for the moment. Worst of all, when I finally got home I would fall into a chair with no energy to play with my two boys. My family got the bad end of the deal. Something needed to change.

Over the next few weeks, I began to make a few small changes to my eating and exercise habits. No major program, just a few basic things. Mostly, I cut out fast food and started running. Predictably, I was soon feeling and looking better.

I've discovered that a short run gets my blood pumping and my brain back on track. I'm able to speak more effectively and am once again the king of the carpet at home.

Even in Sickness

We have to be careful not to confuse health and strength with the lack of sickness. Total health is living to the extreme in spite of your physical conditions. It's breaking physical limits, not living without any physical boundaries. In fact, some of the healthiest people I know have determined to worship God with their bodies in spite of their physical handicaps and limitations. My good friend Dave Hammer is, for me, a picture of total health. As a teenager, Dave loved to play hockey and ride motorcycles. But when he was eighteen, he lost the use of his legs and partial use of his hands when a bullet grazed his spinal cord. He had every reason in the world to stop living, but he determined to "make the most of every opportunity" (Ephesians 5:16). Today Dave is a brilliant entrepreneur and shrewd business owner. And nearly every weekend, he watches his son, David Jr., ride his motorcycle in competition.

My mother-in-law, Susan Roehl, is also a picture for me of total health. And yet consider what she's been through: Forty years ago, after the birth of her first child, she was diagnosed with a rare blood clot condition called Leiden Factor 5. Then at age forty, she learned she had type I (juvenile) diabetes and would have to take insulin every day for the rest of her life. In 1996 she underwent surgery for breast cancer. Three years later, she self-diagnosed Graves' Disease, which the doctors concurred and then prescribed Synthroid for her. To add to the list, she lives every day with osteoporosis and osteoarthritis. She also has a floppy heart valve, high blood pressure, and sleep apnea, which is the weirdest of them all—she gets to wear a Darth Vader–style mask to bed every night to help her breathe.

I would dare say most of us, if we were in her shoes, would have given up somewhere around disease number three or four. A lot of us would stop praying the Word, sink back into self-pity, and either eat or soap opera our way though life. Not Susan Roehl. She fully understands the weight of God's call on her life. Giving up or giving over to the enemy is simply not in her. Although it's tougher for her than most, she's determined to steward her body so God can get as much bang out of it as He wants. She swims at least one mile a minimum of three times per week, and she does it in less than forty minutes. I've tried it with her. Trust me, she's an animal. On the days she isn't swimming, she walks a mile and a half. She's also tenacious about her diet, carefully selecting fiber, fruits, vegetables, and nuts. Talk about Wonder Woman!

Susan, ever the encourager and now in her sixties, still travels the world, plays with her grandkids, and is a prolific e-mailer. There's no wonder that the list of people whose lives she has touched would take up as much space as this entire chapter. I think God honors the way she worships Him with her health. And she's the perfect candidate for Jesus to give the gift of total health. She's demonstrated that she values every aspect of the life God's given her.

As Strong as Ever

God looks down at us in the same loving way that I looked down at little Harrison with hope that he would grow to be strong and full of life. God's desire for us is that we have energy and strength our entire lives. The Scriptures tell us that when his time came to die, Moses "was as strong as ever"

(Deuteronomy 34:7). And God gave this promise to His people through the prophet Isaiah: "The LORD will guide you continually, watering your life when you are dry and keeping you healthy, too. You will be like a well-watered garden, like an ever-flowing spring" (Isaiah 58:11).

The last thing God wants is for us to be sluggish, low on energy, devoid of spunk and spark. Proverbs tells us clearly that God is looking for high-energy ant, not can't-get-out-of-bed slug. Clearly, God wants us to be healthy and strong *in* Him and *for* Him, as He makes clear in His promise: "Those who wait on the LORD will find new strength" (Isaiah 40:31). If we truly wait for Him in faith and hope, we'll then be able to say with Paul, "I can do everything with the help of Christ who gives me the strength I need" (Philippians 4:13).

Your Takeaway

Plot Points

- God made us whole people—body, mind, and spirit. Stewardship of our bodies is as much worship as stewardship of any other part of who we are.
- We're to pursue health and wholeness in this area even in spite of physical diseases and limitations.
- The source of all true strength is God.

Dialogue with a Sage

- Why is total fitness really important?
- How is our physical self connected to our spiritual self?
- What does self-discipline have to do with total health?
- What aspect of your physical health needs the most improvement? What can you do to improve it?

- Are there any harmful habits that may be affecting your total health? What can you do to eliminate these habits?
- What are your specific health goals, particularly in terms of exercise, diet, and sleep?

From the Script

"Give yourselves completely to God since you have been given new life. And use your whole body as a tool to do what is right for the glory of God" (Romans 6:13).

chapter thirteen

SYNERGY

The Hero's Relationships

It just wasn't working. Coach Boone sat alone wondering why he'd ever thought it might. As a black coach in a newly integrated school in Virginia, he seemed to be fighting an uphill battle. His "team" was anything but. The white players refused to play with the new black players, and the black players felt like second-class citizens. The school had kept the old head coach on as assistant coach, which didn't help.

Their preseason football camp in Pennsylvania was supposed to be the time when the team came together. Instead it was coming apart. Unless something happened, it looked like the season and Coach Boone's career would be lost.

A Team Is Born

Then something happened. Deep inside Coach Boone, a spark was lit. He got it. He understood. Early the next morning, he woke the boys up and took them on a run that led them to the historic battlefield of Gettysburg. Here was the place where a critical victory for freedom had been won so long ago. And here, on the mist-shrouded Pennsylvania morning, the coach spilled his guts: "If we don't come together, right now, on this hallowed ground, we too will be destroyed, just like they were. I don't care if you like each other or not, but you will respect each other. And maybe…we'll learn to play this game like men."

It worked. Twenty-one boys had arrived at camp the week before, and twenty-one men left it. After the camp, the Titans played with heart, eventually winning the Virginia state championship and their hometown's heart. *Remember the Titans* is a moving film, and Jerry Bruckheimer brilliantly paints a picture of what happens when a team comes together. It's like *Hoosiers,* when a ragtag, small-town basketball team goes all the way. It's *The Patriot,* when a bunch of farmers win freedom and a nation is born. There's something powerful when a hero realizes he can do far more with others than he could on his own.

That's synergy…and it's perhaps the most powerful secret of the hero.

Together

I was a nerdy fifth grader. Although my mother worked hard to keep me stylish, I wore Coke-bottle glasses, and I think I looked more like a Norman Rockwell character from the cover of *Saturday Evening Post.* I was uncoordinated and more than a bit clumsy, spending most of my spare time outdoors, camping and fishing, rather than playing sports. I was usually the last one to be picked at school for any team. I remember the hot pain of being last in line and last to be chosen. I can't tell you how many times I heard, "I guess we'll take John." Of course, as an eleven-year-old you never show your feelings.

I'd just jump right over to my new team and hope the bell rang before my turn came to bat.

The sting of rejection is one of the most painful anyone can endure. As a youth pastor, I've worked with countless students in the wake of childhood abuse and other varieties of adolescent rejection. I think I might have experienced an incurable wound myself if it hadn't been for Ricky and Mike. Robert South once said that "a true friend is the gift of God, and He only who made hearts can unite them." God must have had something to do with my finding them. These two became my soul mates. Together we built forts, shunned girls, and discovered new neighborhoods. But most of all, when we were together, we were ourselves. These two guys somehow, without even knowing it, were the sponges for my rejection and pain and insecurity. In exchange, I was the same for them. These two friends helped me find my eleven-year-old strength and were the original fellowship that would eventually grow and change and follow me throughout my life. They laughed with me. They encouraged me. They challenged me. When I was with them, I was more.

> God must have had something to do with my finding them.

That, really, is the charge of the body of Christ and the secret of the hero.

There's some mystical secret in relationships the way God created them to work. It happens when a broken vessel pours out, and yet receives love and acceptance and grace in exchange. That's what happened at the cross. Calvary is the garden of broken dreams and new vision. There's some mysterious alchemy in blood and sweat and tears that produces a forever changed and transformed life. At the cross, your life can be so much more than it is now. At the cross, your rejections and pettiness and hurts will collide with His grace. The result is a changed life and a powerful model of synergy.

The cross still stands as the greatest example of genuine relationship. No expectations, no facades. Just plain, unmasked grace and forgiveness and freedom.

God seemed to set it up so our relational barriers are moved when we live for others rather than ourselves. In dying, we live. In giving, we're filled. It's the paradox of God-breathed relationships. A thief becomes the first resident of paradise. A betrayer becomes a cornerstone of the church. When we understand the power of this synergy, we unleash our potential to live truly unlimited lives.

Fractures

I kept a record of my appointments that day.

At 10:00 A.M., I met with Greg Korning. He walked into my office red-faced and loaded. I reached over to close the door behind him and waved my hand toward the small sofa. He declined the offer and we both stood. It was clear he wasn't planning on staying long. He was fed up and furious. For the next ten minutes, he poured out his frustration about his seventeen-year-old son. Out too late. Wrecked the car. Usually high on pot. I'd heard it before. As soon as Greg was finished, he stormed out of my office. He didn't ask me what I thought; he just wanted me to fix it. A relationship left untouched for so long now needed desperate repair. I wondered if the entire engine didn't need replacing.

Jamie was next. As she walked through the door, she headed straight to the sofa. Clearly, she'd been here before. She fell on the sofa, pulled her knees up to her face and broke into tears without even waiting for the door to close. Between sobs I could hear a few words: "I...I don't understand. Why?

Why can't he love me for who I am?" Different guy, same story. Again, a solitary life never needed to be one. Somewhere in the past of this little girl, she or someone around her had the opportunity to fix the flat. Now it would be painful, but all the more important.

Kent was my one o'clock appointment. This was the kind of guy everyone wants to be around. He's funny, good-looking, and seems to have it all. As he walked into my office, he high-fived me, then turned to shut the door. It took almost an hour before he began to open up and tell me why he'd come. In the end, he told me he was deeply depressed and incredibly lonely. His life was one of sports and parties but no real friends. Maybe he's never tried to be a friend. Maybe his dad left a wound that nothing except the cross can heal. Or maybe he simply needs to get over himself and grow up. In any case, his relational wheel is producing no synergy for his life and is actually keeping him from fulfilling God's best in him.

These three are typical of the deep and growing relationship epidemic we seem to be suffering from. What about you? How are your relationships with your family and friends? Do you experience deep, meaningful exchanges with those closest to you? Or are there barriers at the core that seem to keep you from connecting with others?

Our world is full of pain. Read the newspapers, watch the news. It's everywhere. And the most stinging source of pain we can experience usually comes from those we love or who are supposed to love us. Every day, children are ruthlessly abused. Wives and husbands sign away their commitments in divorce papers. And close friends are separated by disloyalty, betrayal, and disillusionment.

Momentum

That's not the way God wants it to be.

Luke 2:52 (NIV) concludes by telling us that Jesus grew "in favor with...men." This implies that He advanced and moved forward and pushed the limits in His relationships. Jesus wasn't a wallflower or a recluse. Any image of Jesus spending His childhood or teenage years in isolation is unfounded. Scripture seems to suggest that He was well-liked and well-adjusted.

Growing in favor with men—does that mean doing whatever it takes to get people to like us?

No, because our life isn't about taking center stage or making everything better for ourselves. As long as we see life exclusively through the lens of our own selves, we'll never experience the full life Jesus promised. God's plan for you and me is to live lives that are wonderfully full and meaningful, but we can never experience the life He has for us until we understand the principle of synergy.

There's a simple physics formula that says momentum equals mass times velocity. Velocity is speed and effort, and mass means people. That's you and me, exerting incredible amounts of effort and running like crazy. Without mass, it's like only a single BB hitting a wall. But *with* mass—with other people—we gain the power of a freight train to move forward. The more mass, the more momentum. That's synergy.

One person can only do so much. Two or more people can do incredibly more. Modern self-help often says the opposite. To a large degree it tells us, "Make life better for *you*, think yourself rich, and mind your own business." I think that's backward. The truth is, two are better than one. As I said before, destiny nearly always comes in pairs.

Jesus' life was never about making friends for His own sake. He committed Himself to loving the unlovely and taking time for the people no one else took time for, because He genuinely loved them. And that's the secret of limitless synergy.

God wants your relationships to be out of the park. He wants your friendships to be genuine and for a lifetime. He wants you to experience freedom with your family and your coworkers and your friends. God wants to totally and completely lift the lid off your social life. But He doesn't want to do it just for your sake. He wants to do it for the sake of the kingdom. You see, God sees the beginning from the end. He understands and sees the final portrait when we may see only the up close piece that's our own life.

A few years ago, I was in Israel and had the opportunity to visit some of the greatest cathedrals in the country. One cathedral in particular stuck in my mind. I remember walking through the front door and seeing a massive mosaic on the floor of the church. The mosaic formed an incredible picture of Mary, the mother of Jesus, holding Him at the foot of the cross. There must have been thousands of small pieces of glass or stone, of all different shapes and colors and sizes. Alone, each piece would mean nothing. But under the care and hand of a master artist, the thousands of fragments became a timeless masterpiece. Each piece was different, but only together did they form the picture of beauty. We're the same way.

Like the people who came to my office that day, we all have our own pain and secret hurts and deep wounds. On our own, we're nothing more than jagged, broken pieces of humanity. But under the hand of God, we can become an incredible picture of love and life and beauty. And that picture happens only when we allow Him to place us together, side by side.

I have a friend who shaved his head when a good buddy was diagnosed with cancer. He was desperate to show his friend that he understood and wanted to feel his pain with him. That's the way God meant our relationships to be.

Social King

Luke made a point of telling us that Jesus grew in favor with man. He could have stated simply that Jesus grew in favor with God and ended it at that. But he didn't, and for good reason. Jesus was unsurpassed in social skills. And He connected with everyone—the rich and poor, healthy and sick, famous and obscure. He was perfectly at home in any social setting. He loved parties. In fact, for His first miracle, Jesus picked a party as the setting—the wedding feast at Cana in Galilee.

The Bible says Jesus and His disciples were invited to the reception. I've often wondered what the bride and groom were thinking as they were preparing their invitations. "Hey, what about that Jesus guy? He's always a blast." "Yeah, and if He comes, He'll bring His friends with Him. That'll get things going."

> Jesus loved parties.

It was at this wedding reception that Jesus turned water into wine. Isn't that amazing? He didn't choose a healing as His first miracle, or stopping a storm or walking on water. No, He chose something much more informal. The wine had run out at the party, and Jesus kept it flowing, which meant a more enjoyable time for everyone there on this social occasion. Jesus understood the importance of connecting with people and serving them in many ways.

So determine today to embrace others and engage one of the most valuable secrets of the hero—the synergy that comes from relationships.

Your Takeaway

Plot Points

- Relationships are the connecting points of life.
- The power of synergy begins to work for you when you connect with others.
- The more strong people there are on your team, the better the team.
- Genuine love for others is the foundation for healthy relationships.

Dialogue with a Sage

- Who are your best friends, and how do they help you most?
- How have your friendships helped you move beyond limitations in your life? How have friends helped you do what you could not do on your own?
- What are the most effective teams of people you have been involved with, and what was the secret of their success?

From the Script

"Now you can have sincere love for each other as brothers and sisters because you were cleansed from your sins when you accepted the truth of the Good News. So see to it that you really do love each other intensely with all your hearts" (1 Peter 1:22).

part four

THE

CONFLICT

chapter fourteen

RULES OF ENGAGEMENT

Understanding Limitations

The hero understands the characters of his epic adventure. He's in search of freedom, full engagement, and a life that embraces the success paradox. His heart and life are surrendered to the King and he walks with the confidence of a man on a mission. He's got the passion of a being spiritually in tune with God, the wisdom and strategy that come from continually exercising his mind, the strength and energy that result from staying physically healthy, and the synergy that flows from strong relationships with others.

That's you—the hero of your epic life. You've begun your journey, but soon you'll be faced with obstacles—limits that stand between you and your goal.

The Bible says, "Do not be surprised at the painful trial you are suffering, as though something strange were happening to you" (1 Peter 4:12, NIV). The hero who encounters conflict knows he's nearer to his goal. So don't be surprised by situations that challenge your current way of thinking or push you out of your comfort zone—that's where you belong.

Have you ever seen a first-birthday party? There's nothing like it. I've watched all three of my own kids turn one and every time I see the same thing. For the Bolins, it's a big deal. It's about a lot more than simply celebrating the first turn of the calendar. It's about their first taste of *chocolate*. Not just a taste, but all they want and any way they want it.

You can see the picture. Tiny hands covered in chocolate cake and chocolate icing, happily cramming as much as possible into a tiny mouth. Of course, most of it ends up on their face and hair and clothes. But then, that's the point. For that one glorious moment, there are no rules. Just plain old "Go nuts!" Food flies, cameras roll, and we all laugh.

I think that's a pretty good picture of the life God intends for us. It's not one of breaking rules and breaking God's heart, but one of living without holding back. You shouldn't be content doing paint-by-number when God created you to splash vibrant color against the canvas of your life. After all, your life is exactly that—a blank canvas waiting for His touch, His plans, His paintbrush. The same God who flung the stars into the sky and who handcrafted the toucan and the orchid and the Rocky Mountains waits to create a masterpiece out of your life.

The Bible says, "No eye has seen, no ear has heard, and no mind has imagined what God has prepared for those who love him" (1 Corinthians 2:9). And yet some people exchange this unimaginable, limitless life He wants for them with a pre-made, store-bought version. Maybe because they're afraid of what their life would look like if they gave it fully to God. Or maybe they've bought into the lie that they've already gone as far as they can go.

God wants us to be totally on fire with life. He wants us to be out of the ordinary, not out of alignment. Living the engaged life is living like Jack London said: with "every atom of me in magnificent glow."

In the Bible, Job's friend Elihu once told him, "Don't you see how God's wooing you from the jaws of danger? How he's drawing you into wide-open places—inviting you to feast at a table laden with blessings?" (Job 36:16, *The Message*). God is doing the same thing for us. He clearly wants us to live free from hurtful limits and restrictions.

But to understand how to do that, we have to better understand what those limits are to begin with, and where they come from. Then we can determine how best to push beyond them.

Good and Bad

The *American Heritage Dictionary* defines a "limit" as 1.) a restriction; and 2.) the greatest or least amount of something allowed. Limits can be thought of as barriers that either keep us restrained to a particular area or inform us how far we can go.

From the time we're born, we grow accustomed to living our lives in and around limits. There are age limits for playing sports, time limits for taking tests, and term limits for political candidates. Limits can be placed on us by God, a government, our parents, our workplace, our churches, and ourselves. They can also be placed on us by the enemy as a direct effort to impede the work of God in our lives.

> Some limits are healthy; others are destructive at their core.

Some limits are good and healthy, while others are destructive at their core. Other limits are neutral, neither good nor bad, yet still necessary. God knows when limits are not only helpful, but critical. He gave us an age limit of 120 years (Genesis 6:3). He put a border around the Promised Land, and He had very specific limits in the Garden of Eden (Genesis 2:17). God establishes such limits for us because He knows what's best for us.

Many of the laws handed down by our government are concerned with setting limits on our lives. Arguably, some of these may be good and some bad, but we're to obey them nonetheless (see Titus 3:1).

Speed limits, for example, keep us safe on the highways, as do roadblocks and detours. Just the other day I was traveling in the mountains when I was slowed by a construction barrier in the road. The road seemed clear and unobstructed and I was tempted to ignore the warnings. Annoyed, I followed a detour that went parallel to the road I wanted to be on. A couple of miles later I saw an overturned car in the middle of a half-dozen police and fire rescue vehicles. *A good barrier after all,* I thought as I drove on.

Another way to think of limitations is as "boundaries." Author John Townsend says that boundaries define who we are: "They define what is me and what is not me." He's right. Learning when to say yes and when to say no ultimately determines the scope of our lives. Jesus told us, "Simply let your 'Yes' be 'Yes,' and your 'No,' 'No'; anything beyond this comes from the evil one" (Matthew 5:37, NIV). There's a lot of value in establishing limits and boundaries in relationships and convictions.

So the whole concept of limits is a complex one. And as we go through life, it often becomes more and more difficult to differentiate between healthy limits and boundaries and those that are destructive. A lot of people have been fooled into accepting a particular restriction when in fact it's a destructive limit whose roots are in guilt, fear, or greed. They stop at a boundary line that's not from God, one that limits their life and potential. And that's why I've written this book.

I want to expose for you the limits that might be keeping you from becoming the person God created you to be. They're negative and destructive to you as a hero in God's great epic. My passion is to help you smash down the negative limiting forces in your life so you can live a free, fully engaged life in Christ.

Limited Thinking

Where do negative limits come from? Some come from simply being part of a fallen world, while others are imposed on us by ourselves. Ultimately, all these negative limits find their root in our enemy, the villain in our life's epic story. Remember what Jesus said about him: "He was a murderer from the beginning and has always hated the truth. There is no truth in him. When he lies, it is consistent with his character; for he is a liar and the father of lies" (John 8:44). The negative limits that Satan brings our way are, in essence, illusions. They're figments of our imaginations and emotions. The villain of our lives loves to concoct fantasies about who we are and what we should do. Generally, they're fabrications about what we can and cannot do based on our past pain, our present realities, or our future fears.

> The lion's share of these limits are self-imposed.

Negative limits can exist in any area of our lives—we face physical, mental, spiritual, and relational limits. The lion's share of these limits are self-imposed, the products of our own doubts, fears, and lack of belief. But whether we're victims purely of our own attitudes and decisions or we're prey to a deeper, darker enemy, the main battlefield where we encounter these dangerous limits is our minds. It's in our minds that we fight to believe God can accomplish great things in us, or else we give in to the lie that He can't use us.

Thomas Dreier wrote that "the life each of us lives is the life within the limits of our own thinking. To have life more abundant, we must think in limitless terms of abundance."

I'm not talking about simply getting a positive mental attitude and repeating an emotionally charged mantra every morning for a month. I'm not talking about visualization or imagination. I'm talking about changing our minds—doing a one-eighty in the way we think about limits. Unless we change the way our minds process limitations, we'll continue to respond the way we always have, and nothing will change at all. This is one of the reasons why so many people will read great books and get energized and motivated but never see any sustainable life change. They change the information in their head, but they never change their minds.

The Invisible Wall

A group of marine scientists once conducted a series of experiments with a tank full of barracuda. At first, they fed these fish their favorite food, live mackerel, every day for a month. Of course, the aggressive fish would devour the mackerel in an instant. Then the scientists placed a clear glass panel between the barracuda and the bait fish. As soon as the mackerel were lowered into the tank, the barracuda immediately moved toward them, smashing their noses on the clear glass.

The predators continued to attempt to get past the glass until, finally, they realized their efforts were futile. Then the scientists removed the glass and allowed the mackerel to freely swim. The mackerel, of course, stayed behind the perceived wall. And the barracuda, with nothing standing between them and their prey, contentedly stayed on their side of the tank.

The wall was gone. The barrier had been removed, but the fish still stayed in their newly created "cage." All the food the barracuda could stomach was just waiting to be eaten, but was never touched. The false barrier of past hurt kept the fish from making any move at all.

And that's just like us, isn't it? Though a life without limits awaits us, we often allow past hurts and mistakes to keep us from taking full advantage of it.

A good friend of mine was eager to share with me his experience at a weekend retreat, which he'd attended a few months earlier, so I scheduled a lunch with him to find out what had happened. For an hour, Dan unfolded moment by moment what sounded like the most impacting three-day retreat I'd ever heard of. I found myself wishing I'd been there. He told me the retreat had changed his life. And I believe it almost had.

Dan left the retreat with a new leash on life, with a new passion for his future and a new love for his wife. He had a renewed commitment to God and a path consistent with his newly discovered identity. But the more we talked, the more I began to realize Dan had dropped the ball. His relationship with his wife had stayed the same, and his job had stayed the same. His passion was still strong, but it was beginning to fade. Why?

As we talked, I discovered that Dan had an invisible wall of past hurt and failure that kept him from moving out. Though he had all the components of a great life waiting for him, he was constrained to his little side of the tank, not realizing how close his dreams were. The glass barrier or limit in his life had been there so long, it had begun to affect his mind.

Bad habits of negative thought will only reinforce limits in your life, in your relationships, and in your walk with God.

They're the negative things we say and believe so many times that they become part of our core. We begin to really believe them, and even begin to make small changes to accommodate our made-up reality. If someone believes and says repeatedly that he'll always be broke, he'll have trouble ever getting out of debt. We are what we think. If a person says and acts as though he'll never have meaningful relationships, he'll find it difficult to make friends. And if a person constantly reinforces that he's tired and overworked and out of time, chances are he'll end up tired, overworked, and with no extra time for anything except complaining.

Think About This

"People see what they are prepared to see," Emerson asserted. He was right. The barracuda were prepared to encounter a glass pane between them and their meal, and my friend Dan was prepared to encounter the same pain and failure he'd encountered before.

So what's the solution?

The Bible tells us about a much better way of mental reinforcement: "Whatever is true, whatever is noble, whatever is right, whatever is pure, whatever is lovely, whatever is admirable—if anything is excellent or praiseworthy—think about such things" (Philippians 4:8, NIV). The only way to get over a bad belief system, change your paradigm, and begin to break barriers is to turn to God and His Word. Trying on your own to transform your mind will be nothing more than an exercise in self. Realizing that no matter how hard you try, you're successful only in and through the Lord...that's what will lead to bursting your mental limits.

Jacob discovered it after surrendering to the touch of God while wrestling with the angel. Jonah found it after yielding to God's purposes while trapped in the belly of a whale. And Paul realized it only after he'd been struck blind. Each of them experienced a new level of limitless living after they encountered God. He has a way of showing up and changing us when we've come to the end of ourselves. It's just the way He is.

The Wine of Possibility

So what can you do *practically* to make the mental shift?

First, you've got to examine your life and be sure you've given Christ lordship. That means identifying any distraction or misdirection of your heart and getting in line with the King's heart.

Second, you've got to examine your thinking and consider the source of any doubt or fear about your future. This will require meditating on the Word of God and resisting the villain.

Third, you've got to deal with your past, your "backstory." By understanding why certain limits have developed in our minds, we can better discover how to fully live beyond them. (We'll look more at this issue later.)

Jesus said, "Anything is possible if a person believes" (Mark 9:23)—not simply reads or hears, but believes. Do you believe anything is possible in your life?

"If I were to wish for anything," the philosopher Søren Kierkegaard said, "I should not wish for wealth and power, but for the passionate sense of the potential, for the eye which, ever young and ardent, sees the possible... What wine is so sparkling, what so fragrant, what so intoxicating, as possibility!"

Plot Points

- Limits can be healthy, harmful, or neutral.
- Negative limits can exist in any area of our lives.
- All negative limits find their root in the villain's lies.
- Bad habits of negative thought will reinforce negative limits in our lives.

Dialogue with a Sage

- What are the biggest limits you've faced in your life? How have you overcome them, or how have they affected you if you were unable to overcome them?
- Does God ever limit us? If so, in what ways?
- How do we limit God from moving in our lives?

From the Script

Jesus said: "With man this is impossible, but with God all things are possible" (Matthew 19:26, NIV).

chapter fifteen

ALIENS AT WAR

Accepting the Call to Battle

Christians are boring." Brandon's words echoed in my head as I pulled out of the restaurant parking lot. Brandon, who was seventeen, had agreed to meet me for a cup of coffee. Of course, he hadn't asked for the meeting. His parents, desperate to fix years of bad decisions, had hoped for a bit of youth pastor pixie dust. Even though I knew it simply didn't exist, I decided to take the time with him anyhow.

As a youth pastor, I'd dealt with hundreds of difficult students. Felons, drug addicts, the clinically depressed. I figured this kid would add to my list.

But Brandon wasn't at all what I'd expected. He was good-looking, intelligent, athletic, and articulate. As we laughed and talked, I began to realize this wasn't the out-of-control kid his parents had described. This was the kind of guy I wanted in our youth group. In fact, this was the kind of guy I wanted as a friend. As our conversation came to an end, I asked him why he hadn't considered Christianity. His answer was simple: "Because Christians are boring." I wasn't sure what to say.

Of course, at first I defended Christian kids, Christian music, and Christian movies as best I could. But in the end, I really had no argument. The truth is, Brandon seemed to be right. And I hated it. Why is it that Christians have gotten the reputation for being boring and out of touch? Is that what we are? Nice, ordered, and absurdly even?

I know Christians who are delightfully funny. Others are deeply wise and melancholy. Still others are off-the-charts outgoing and wild. My friend Christopher is the furthest thing from being a boring Christian that I've ever met. We've been friends for over ten years now, and he's always been that way. Christopher lives on the edge. It's where he feels most alive. In the past twelve months alone he's been investigated by the FBI, dropped by a helicopter into a jungle, chased out of a shower by a swarm of bees in New Guinea, dodged land mines in Afghanistan, and nearly fell in love in Alabama.

No, Christians aren't boring. But I dare say many of them are more than a bit bored. How many Sunday afternoon potlucks, endless song services, and turgid Bible study groups can you endure? Be polite. Be nice. Read your Bible. Wait your turn. Don't push. Don't fight. Don't cuss.

But if you're like me, you know there has to be more to being a Christian than following a list of what to do or not do. And this something more has to do with a battle.

We're Not Just Passing Through

Maybe you've seen the Christian bumper sticker that reads, "I'm just passing through"—as if we're on a lifelong senior citizen bus tour of the Grand Canyon. Once again, boring. Isn't there something in you that wants to jump off the bus and explore? Walk to the edge of the canyon? Or even venture down into the canyon itself? It's true, this isn't our home, but I can assure you, God hasn't placed you on

Planet Earth so you could "just pass through." He's sent you here to be His ambassador, His representative, His agent. Whether you know it or not, whether you like it or not, you're here on a mission. A fighting mission.

When I was a kid, I used to have a recurring dream that the world was filled with aliens, including my parents and especially my sisters. I imagined I was one of only a few real humans alive and I was on a secret mission to rescue those few. What if I told you that you, too, are a secret agent? And that you've been placed here for a purpose? And what if I told you there are aliens all around you? Or…that *you* are the alien?

> I imagined I was on a secret rescue mission.

Peter said that as Christians we're "aliens and strangers in the world" (1 Peter 2:11, NIV). That means first that we aren't from here and this isn't our final destination. It also means we're not alone. This world is occupied by others who like us are on a spiritual journey.

But this planet is also occupied territory for a much darker and more sinister race, hell-bent on crashing the bus and destroying us. The Bible calls them the evil powers of this world. It's the prince of this world and his demons—the villain and his army. There's a real force out there determined to block the plan of God for your life. Paul reminded us that we "do not wrestle against flesh and blood, but against principalities, against powers, against the rulers of the darkness of this age" (Ephesians 6:12, NKJV). Sounds a lot like a scene from *The Lord of the Rings,* doesn't it?

The Battle Begins

This life is a battle. Like it or not, you're surrounded by an all-consuming conflict. The villain has already declared total war, and surrender for him is not an option. It will be a fight to the death, and a war involving every human being.

Right now we're all lined up, and the King and the villain are picking their teams. And then…*your* name is called. But not just by one captain. Both the King and the villain have selected you, and you have a choice to make.

Staying in line isn't an option. We try to think it is, but really it's not. "Anyone who isn't helping me opposes me," Jesus said, "and anyone who isn't working with me is actually working against me" (Matthew 12:30). The default team for those of us who fail to take sides is always with the villain. If we stay neutral, the villain wins.

And that's his plan—to keep you from taking the side of the King. He has already begun building strongholds to keep you locked in, barred up, and pushed back. He loves to watch daring Christians become bored, so he downplays the epic battle that's as real as this book in your hands.

He tells us instead that it's okay to be average, it's okay to be a nobody. He whispers in our ear: "Everything's fine the way it is. You don't have to prove anything to anybody. So don't rock the boat, don't do anything out of the ordinary. Do what everyone else does. Do what everyone expects." He doesn't really know God's plan for your life, but he's hot on the path to try to derail and distract you from accomplishing it, whatever it is.

Don't let him. You've got to beat him at his game and strike first.

More than Just "Nice"

As a kid, I never hit another kid in the face. In fact, I can remember only one time in my life I've actually, really hit any-one. I was in fifth grade and agreed to meet Mike, the class bully, in the parking lot after school. During recess, he teased Cathy Ingham, the girl of my dreams, so I challenged him to a duel to protect Cathy's honor. The brawl didn't last long and ended in a draw, but I've always regretted not hitting Mike in the face. I had the opportunity, but I cowered. I regret it simply because that's how I've lived—like a really, really nice guy.

Author John Eldredge asks, "Did you ever dream of becoming a nice guy?" In your dreams, were you a yes-man or a fierce knight? Were you the homely wallflower or the beautiful princess? Typically, "nice" men and women are eaten alive on the battlefield of the enemy. Our Christian life has got to move far beyond "nice" if we're going to be successful in the battle we face.

The other day, I was in a meeting with my pastor, talking about a few tough decisions I have to make. As we discussed the difficult choices facing me, I seemed to be at an impasse. The temptation to take an easy way out was stronger than I'd like to admit. And it even made sense. For a while, we tossed around a few less painful options. Then suddenly, right there, I knew what I had to do. I actually said, "I've never hit a kid in the face, and I've got to do it." I knew I had to face Goliath. It was time for me to stop making excuses and call a spade a spade.

I've done that. And in doing it, I've taken sides.

The Lord Jesus once rebuked the people in a certain church for their lukewarmness, and warned them that it would lead to God's rejection of them: "So, because you are lukewarm—neither hot nor cold—I am about to spit you out of my mouth" (Revelation 3:16, NIV). In accepting average, they were in essence choosing the wrong side.

Jesus has no place for apathetic followers—for tepid, nice, average, just-passing-through Christians.

The Line Is Drawn

So the line in the sand has been drawn. On one side is adventure; on the other side is average.

Right now, the forces of heaven are lined up and ready to face down the soldiers of hell. You have a place on God's side in this battle. There's an empty slot, right next to Jesus. Your weapons are there, lying on the ground. Your armor fits perfectly. The hosts of heaven are ready for the great battle, and right now, they're calling for you to join them.

And so is the villain.

Make no mistake about it. God has cast His vote for you—and so has the villain.

> God has cast His vote for you—and so has the villain.

So you have a choice to make. Don't do what I once did, and pull your punches. Instead, go ahead and hit the enemy in the face. Leap out and show your strength. Say good-bye to average, and be the man of valor or the woman of courage God has made you to be.

But I've got to warn you, when you stop accepting average and start living like you're here for a reason, you'll suddenly find yourself facing some new struggles. If you've determined to reject average and to live fully engaged in every area of life, then I can tell you that the enemy is furious. He isn't going to just roll over and allow you to do a victory dance on him. You can count on him to throw another wave of attack against you.

But never fear. In this battle, you have in your possession and at your disposal the most powerful secret weapon anyone could ever imagine. What is it?

It's this: your knowledge and confident faith that the battle is, in total fact, already won.

I know you're out there. I can feel you now. I know that you're afraid. You're afraid of us. You're afraid of change. I don't know the future. I didn't come here to tell you how this is going to end. I came here to tell you how it's going to begin. I'm going to hang up this phone and then I'm going to show these people what you don't want them to see. I'm going to show them a world without you, a world without rules and controls, without borders or boundaries, a world where anything is possible. Where we go from there is a choice I leave to you.

That's the closing monologue to the movie *The Matrix,* and it's worth thinking about at this point in your epic journey. In *The Matrix,* the enemy has been beaten. Not completely destroyed yet, but put on notice.

Through His death and resurrection, the victory Christ won over Satan and his demons was crushing and complete. The Bible tells us that by His death, Jesus was able to "destroy him who holds the power of death—that is, the devil" (Hebrews 2:14, NIV). That's why He came to this world: "The reason the Son of God appeared was to destroy the devil's work" (1 John 3:8, NIV).

Jesus kept hold of this purpose. And when the time for His crucifixion drew near, He could say confidently, "The time of judgment for the world has come, when the prince of this world will be cast out" (John 12:31). On the night of the Last Supper, just hours before His arrest and trial and torture, Jesus told His disciples who it was that was really being put on trial and sentenced to destruction: "The prince of this world now stands condemned" (John 16:11 NIV).

Destroyed, cast out, and condemned—that's total defeat for the villain and his forces, all because of the cross of Christ. And that defeat was as humiliating as it was complete: God "stripped all the spiritual tyrants in the universe of their sham authority at the Cross and marched them naked through the streets" (Colossians 2:15, *The Message*). What happened for us at the cross was the climactic fulfillment of what was foreshadowed centuries before when Pharaoh's forces drowned in the Red Sea while trying to capture God's people—God "saved them from the hand of the foe; from the hand of the enemy he redeemed them" (Psalm 106:10, NIV).

Through the work of Christ, our enemy, the villain, has already been totally trounced. In the end, he'll be utterly destroyed in hell (see Revelation 20:10). In the meantime, God in His wisdom is allowing Satan limited influence and movement—our enemy's out there, still trying to steal what God has planted in your heart. Don't let him. When he speaks lies to you, speak back God's Word.

No Plan Thwarted

There's a verse in the Bible where someone says to God, "I know that you can do all things; no plan of yours can be thwarted." Do you know who said that? It wasn't someone enjoying what we would consider the good life. It wasn't one of the patriarchs who'd just seen the awesome hand of God open an ocean or stop the sun or rain manna from heaven.

No, it was a guy with his back against a wall. Job was suffering on every side. His painful backstory was happening so fast, it was being written in shorthand. Job was wrestling with the meaning of all the suffering he was going through, and his friends with their lengthy explanations and advice did not seem to have the answers.

Then suddenly, out of a storm, God spoke to Job in powerful, convicting words (see Job chapters 38–41), helping Job finally realize that His plans always trump human understanding. It was then that Job acknowledged before God that He's always free to do whatever He wants, that no plan of His can ever be hindered.

Then in worship Job added, "Therefore I despise myself and repent in dust and ashes" (Job 42:2, 6, NIV). Job's worst struggles—suffering that was probably far worse than anything you or I could imagine—led to deep self-awareness, deep repentance, deep worship, and a deep understanding that God is the true and sovereign Victor who's totally and unshakably in charge of our lives.

Victory Promises

"The help of man is worthless" (Psalm 60:11, NIV). But you have something far beyond the help of man. You have the authority and protection of the Mighty One. Jesus said, "I have given you authority to trample on snakes and scorpions and to overcome all the power of the enemy; nothing will harm you" (Luke 10:19, NIV).

"Resist the Devil," God's Word promises, "and he will flee from you" (James 4:7). It doesn't say "he might flee" or "we hope he'll flee." It says he will run, blaze a trail, take a hike. He'll be furious, but he'll still flee.

Remember what Isaiah acknowledged before God: "The enemy runs at the sound of your voice" (Isaiah 33:3).

To erase "average" and "boring" from your life's vocabulary, there's nothing like going into real battle. Especially when the war is as big as this one is—and especially when you know your side has already won.

In fact, the victory feast is already planned. And the best

way to start celebrating is by staying brave and strong in the final, mop-up battles that still remain.

Your Takeaway

Plot Points

- War is reality in the spiritual world we live in.
- Jesus has no place for apathetic followers who will not actively choose to be on His side in the battle.
- Christ has already won total victory over Satan.
- For the time being, God in His wisdom is allowing Satan limited influence and movement in our lives.

Dialogue with a Sage

- Do you approach daily life with battle-mindedness?
- What helps you most to remember the spiritual conflict we're engaged in?
- What is your responsibility in this spiritual conflict?
- What are the specific choices you need to make at this time in order to serve on Christ's side in the spiritual war of the universe?

From the Script

"Bless the LORD, who is my rock. He gives me strength for war and skill for battle" (Psalm 144:1).

chapter sixteen

UNCOVERING THE BACKSTORY

Freedom from Your Past

While I'm confident to the core that God desires for us to live as fully as we're able, I also know this life is full of pain. Just as Jesus promised that He came to give us full lives, He also promised that we would suffer. There's a place for pain in the pages of our story—a big place.

One of my favorite scenes in *The Lion King* is when the wise old baboon, Rafiki, helps Simba the lion realize that he has to go back to the troubled country of his childhood.

Simba protests, "But going back means I'll have to face my past. I've been running from it for so long."

At this point, Rafiki whacks Simba on the head with his staff.

"Oww!" Simba shouts. "What was that for?"

"It doesn't matter," Rafiki replies. "It's in the past!"

"Yeah, but it still hurts."

"Oh yes, the past can hurt," Rafiki agrees. "But the way I see it, you can either run from it or learn from it."

Rafiki is right; sometimes our past continues to hurt. It's

the shadow that follows us—until we finally turn and face it.

It's what screenwriters call the backstory. The backstory is made up of the people and events that motivate the central figure to action. It's all the stuff that was going on in the characters' lives before the movie's first scene.

For many people, the pain from the past keeps them barred in with fear. But the true hero, rather than allowing the pain to control him and keep him locked in, will turn the tide on it. He pulls the ultimate switcheroo in the face of the villain's plans. The epic hero turns pain from the past into motivation, as William Wallace does in *Braveheart,* and as Maximus does in *Gladiator.* You can, too.

We can learn something from a baboon after all. God's design for us is that we learn from our past, but not live in our past.

The Things We Want to Forget

In all our life stories there are chapters we might like to forget or flip past or erase altogether. They're the dark pages when our worst self mutinied against the King or when someone else's worst self found expression against us. Sometimes these pages seem to go on and on like a slow burning coal, and sometimes they're short bursts, like a red-hot cannon shot.

> Our painful past brings meaning to the rest of our story as nothing else can.

These pages of pain might be filled with the story of the loss of a loved one or a love that was lost. They could be stories of abuse or rejection or disillusionment. Or maybe addiction or a secret sin. We cannot ignore them, for they won't be ignored. If we try to push them away, they'll only emerge at the most inopportune time to haunt us and force us to deal with them.

It would be easy to resent these chapters, and most of us do. But these chapters bring depth and meaning and hope to the rest of our story as nothing else can. Because of them, there's true sweetness in the final victory. And in fact, it's their reality that can trigger the most potent motivation to fight for that victory.

Although I hesitate to talk about those chapters in my own life, it would be impossible for me to truly offer you hope without unveiling at least a bit of my own backstory.

Insecurity at Home

I grew up in a family that looked perfect on the outside: Mom and Dad and six children growing up together in a house on Ellison Avenue in Omaha, Nebraska. We had everything except the picket fence (which didn't matter much, since our only immediate neighbors were Grandma and Grandpa, who lived next door).

For the most part, Mom and Dad were involved in our lives, careful to attend our important functions and to give advice as we needed it, which was often. Our family was well-off, and I remember taking fantastic vacations together (some of my fondest memories). I can't tell you how many times my friends told me, "I wish I had a family like yours. You're so lucky." *If they only knew,* I'd think to myself.

I used to think our trouble started somewhere during my freshman year in high school, but I now know that it began much earlier. As is true for all of us, my story really begins with my parents' stories. My mother is an immigrant from Latvia who moved to the United States in 1950. My father was born into a wealthy Chicago family, thanks to his grandfather, a brilliant inventor and entrepreneur.

They met each other at an acting school at the

Goodman Theatre in downtown Chicago. Like a scene from *The Great Gatsby* or *My Fair Lady*, two unlikely worlds clashed, and passion was the result. The man of means falls for the daughter of an immigrant. The artist is swept off her feet by the scholar-philosopher. The two were married, and the passion continued through thirty years and the raising of six children.

But somewhere between the theater days in Chicago and the long winter nights in Omaha, something haunting or hurtful in their past came back with a fury. The spats began when I was still in elementary school. Through my high school years, the arguing slowly grew louder and more frequent. My pillow would muffle their voices as I cried myself to sleep on countless nights.

My sisters and brother and I were determined to keep the Bolin facade as strong as possible, but in the process I struggled. I could only take so much, and I felt myself slipping into chronic insecurity. I suppose this is partly why God was so real to me during my high school years. I needed Him. I could be real with Him.

I remember one particular December evening when the fighting from their bedroom was louder than usual. Not wanting them to hear my parents argue, I remember moving my little brother and sister downstairs. I wanted to be a knight for my brother and sister, and so that night I determined to stand up to my father for once in my life.

When I did, I was quickly shunned and pushed out of the room. No match for my dad, I ran away to the place I usually sought when I needed to escape. I went outside. In the freezing cold, I stood in the backyard and threw rocks at the silhouettes in that upstairs window. Without even knowing it, they were tearing down my world. I wanted to stand up, but I felt as though I had nothing to stand on.

To be fair, I must say that Dad came and found me in the field across the street from my house and walked me back home. Even through these difficult days, my dad managed to remain my hero and my mom my greatest support.

That was my first page of pain. Years have passed, and thankfully, I'm seeing that God is healing the wound I suffered. It isn't an easy process nor an instant one, but God is faithful through it all. Even now, He's healing the tear between each of my parents and me. And I believe the wounds that were inflicted somewhere in their own backstories are being healed as well. And for this I'm grateful and forever hopeful.

The Sting of a Love Lost

When I was sixteen—in the middle of those years of my insecurity at home—a brown-haired, brown-eyed girl came into my life and quickly became the focus of my valiant heart.

She instantly became my Guinevere. Fatherless, she gave me the opportunity to be for her the noble, protecting knight I'd wanted to be for my own family.

For four years, she was my world. We did everything together. I was there for her dance recitals and her sister's birthday parties. I adopted her mom as sort of a second mom to me.

I'd never loved anyone like I loved her, and for the first time in my life I understood poetry and music. I was certain I'd discovered true love, that we were destined to be married, and that we'd spend the rest of our lives together.

After high school, we enrolled in the same college, and for the first semester there, everything was going according to the romance I'd scripted in my head.

That spring, she went overseas for a semester in Spain, and when she returned, everything seemed different. The spark had left her eye and I sensed the end was near. On a tear-filled night, she told me she'd met someone else in Spain. Although she wanted to salvage our relationship, my heart deeply ached. Once again I felt my feet slipping. Nothing, it seemed was secure. Not wanting to be the one rejected, I took the first opportunity to end our relationship.

A year later, I met my true love, Sarah, who quickly became my very best friend. I've been married for ten wonderful years. Unquestionably, God has redeemed my high school longings and wounded heart with a lifelong friend and lover.

The Wound of a Friend

Another chapter of pain came just as I was beginning my journey into manhood. I was in my early twenties and newly married. This time, the pain was inflicted not by a stranger or a love, but by a close friend, Andy. I'd been out of college for several years, and my truest friends were living states away. Hungry for camaraderie and friendship, I quickly latched on to Andy. Here was someone with whom I could explore the depths of human struggle and the heights of God's kingdom. We laughed together, prayed together, and even killed spiritual giants together. So when the wound came, I was again totally caught off guard.

The line between friendship and betrayal is a fine one, and I found myself awkwardly balancing on a wire. In the end, my feet slipped once again as the wire was pulled out from under me. The horrifying sense of falling was magnified now that I wasn't exactly a boy anymore. The arrow had pierced a sensitive spot, and for several years the wound ached even as it healed. Almost as if reliving my high school years, I felt

> The line between friendship and betrayal is a fine one.

lonely, frustrated, and disillusioned. But the healing began.

A year ago, nearly four years after Andy's arrow landed, I took a retreat to the mountains with the express intention of pulling it out from my heart. That weekend, I wrestled with God. I cried and prayed and struggled with the arrow, until ultimately I gave up…and then God easily popped it out. That's generally how it works. That's not to say I'm totally healed. I'm far from that. But I'm on my way to restoration, and that's a good place to be.

The Pain of Failure

Another chapter that brought some soreness to my soul had to do with my business career. After graduating from college in 1992, I enjoyed a very successful job with the now infamous accounting and consulting firm Arthur Andersen. I was hired as a regional marketing coordinator in the Carolinas and found myself jetting around the country, working with brilliant Ivy League graduates, and power-lunching with multimillionaires. In spite of the seeming success of my job at Andersen, I distinctly remember the overwhelming entrepreneurial urge I had during my two years in the job. I simply wasn't a company man, and I was determined to start my own business one day. In fact, I remember spending many lunch hours in the downtown Charlotte public library researching what business I was going to pioneer.

In 1994, my wife, Sarah, and I packed up a U-Haul truck and said our good-byes to our friends in Charlotte and at Andersen. We had decided to start a mail-order catalog for outdoor sporting goods. We figured Colorado was as good a place as any to run an outdoor business, although we had no friends or job waiting for us there. We ended up in Colorado Springs, and in the summer of 1994 released the first issue of our catalog, *Expedition Quality*. For the next year, we learned the ropes of the direct mail business, mailing over five hundred thousand catalogs to some three dozen countries. The sales began to pour in, and we knew we were in business. And then, just when the wind was picking up in our sail, tragedy struck and the wind was knocked out of us.

A series of bad management decisions on my part had put the company in serious jeopardy. Poor judgment in selecting one of my managers led to embezzlement and ended up costing us the company. In 1996, we sold the remains of the business to a local business owner, but made so little on the sale of the company that Sarah and I were forced to declare bankruptcy a year later.

I felt like an extreme failure. I'd always been driven to succeed, and for the most part, I always had. Now I was experiencing the cold knife of failure, and I didn't like it.

I remember waking up one night in a cold sweat, dreading the future that I'd so foolishly put in jeopardy for Sarah and our children. And that might have been the end of my story, had Sarah not convinced me to ignore the lie of failure that was trying to destroy me. That night she sat up with me, reminding me of the successes of the flopped mail-order venture. She encouraged me to believe all the books I'd read and quoted over the years. In fact, she made me believe our family's future rested not on my success or failure, but on my response to it. She was right. How we respond to pain or failure is more important than the pain or failure to begin with.

Getting Back on the Bike

As I'm writing this, Sarah and I are house-sitting for some good friends of ours for a couple of weeks while they're on family vacation. At least once a month, we spend the good part of an afternoon with them, cooking out, playing volley-ball, or just sitting on the deck talking and laughing. The Blahas have seven children, and the two youngest, Zack and Ben, play great older brothers for our kids. Our boys, especially Harrison, have been talking about spending time at the Blahas' house for a few weeks now. And the one thing Harrison was looking forward to more than anything else was sleeping in Zack and Ben's bunk bed.

I was writing late last night when Sarah heard a little boy's cry coming from downstairs. We quickly rushed down to find Harrison standing over the toilet with a flashlight in his hands and his nose and mouth covered in blood. Somehow, he had bumped his face crawling down from the upper bunk, and that began the avalanche of sobs, blood, and tears.

"Mommy, I was calling for you and you didn't come," he said, exasperated and still crying. "I was scared, so I came down by myself…and that made my nose bleed." He was a heartbreaking sight, but we cleaned him up and asked him if he wanted to sleep with us for the rest of the night. He did. Before he drifted off to sleep, he said he thought he'd just sleep on the lower bunk with Chandler for the rest of the week.

But this morning everything seems to have changed. Harrison woke up bright-eyed, ready for another day of throwing sticks and exploring forests—and he let me know he was planning on sleeping on the top bunk again tonight. Had he so quickly forgotten last night's bloodshed? Had he forgotten the pain and agony and fear that gripped him just a few hours before? Apparently so. To be a child again! Those were the days when one minute you fell and scraped your knee and the next you were back on your bike. When bumps and bruises were quickly forgotten in light of more important adventures to be had.

To Harrison, the pain of falling off the bunk bed was quickly forgotten. That was yesterday and this is today. Seems oversimplified, and yet one of the greatest limiting forces in your life is failing to get free from the weight of your past.

Time to Get Up and Go

Jesus said that God sent Him to earth "to preach deliverance to the captives" (Luke 4:18, NKJV). That means we don't have to be captive any longer to our past circumstances or pain. We don't have to allow the insecurities of our backstory to write the script of our future. Jesus also said He came to heal the brokenhearted. That's what Jesus does best.

I love the story in John 5 where Jesus encountered the sick man sitting at the Pool of Bethesda. This guy had been waiting there for thirty-eight years, hoping to be healed. (Popular belief held that when the waters in the pool were agitated, an angel was stirring the waters, and the first person into the pool at that moment would be healed.) So this guy had lots of time to listen to the enemy's voice whispering in his ear. And for thirty-eight years, the enemy kept this guy in bondage, totally limited physically.

> Do you want to be healed of all the stuff in your past?

He probably would have stayed that way, had it not been for Jesus. Quickly sizing up the situation, Jesus asked this man, "Would you like to get well?" (John 5:6).

In response, the sick man didn't say, "Yes, I would. Please heal me!" Instead he revealed his frustration at being too slow to beat others into the pool when the waters were stirred. He was simply repeating what the enemy had been whispering to him for all those years: *You can't do it. You'll never get healed. Blame someone else.*

Then Jesus said to him, "Stand up, pick up your sleeping mat, and walk" (v. 8). Jesus didn't assign a disciple to him as a lifeguard and dunker. He didn't give the man instructions on how to make it into the pool faster. He gave the man what he really wanted. Deep inside, what he wanted wasn't someone to blame, it was freedom.

God is also asking you and me, "Do you want to be healed of all the stuff in your past?" How do we respond? Usually with excuses or by blaming others. But listen again to what Jesus commanded the sick man: "Get up!" He wants us to stop focusing on our past, and letting it haunt us or keep us pinned down. He wants us to receive healing, and then GET UP AND GO!

Because the Old Is Gone

Now's the time for you to face the dark chapters of your story and lay them at the foot of the cross. And once you've left them there, don't try and pick them back up. Remember, your old self—frustrated and insecure—is gone at Calvary. The new you can take up your position with Christ: "Those who become Christians become new persons. They are not the same anymore, for the old life is gone. A new life has begun!" (2 Corinthians 5:17). Jesus paid the price for every bit of our pain and suffering.

That's why Paul said he had to put everything he had into pushing past it: "I am still not all I should be, but I am focusing all my energies on this one thing: Forgetting the past and looking forward to what lies ahead" (Philippians 3:13). *All* of his energies. The past is a powerful enemy to the unlimited life, but it can be faced and overcome.

Jesus said, "Anyone who puts a hand to the plow and then looks back is not fit for the Kingdom of God" (Luke

9:62). He was emphasizing the importance of letting go of the past and not allowing it to dominate our future.

The chains of your past can be broken, once and for all. They don't have to keep you bound up and held back. They don't have to dominate your decisions or cloud your thinking. Jesus bled and died to pay the price not only for your sin, but also for your pain. He alone can truly forgive and heal.

This is the incredible power of the cross. Because of it, God not only forgives our past mistakes, but the Bible says He also forgets them. He tells us, "I—yes, I alone—am the one who blots out your sins for my own sake and will never think of them again" (Isaiah 43:25). You and I don't usually forgive and forget as He does. Forgetting a past sin usually takes us much longer, and only after a tough process. But God absolutely tosses it out. When we bring it up, it's almost like He says, "What are you talking about?"

Rest with Me

It's easy to tell someone, "Don't let failure get you down," or "Just keep on trying." Life just isn't that simple. Failure can be incredibly devastating and depressing. The night I woke up in a cold sweat thinking about my financial trouble, the idea of "failing forward" seemed miles away. Right then, I just needed someone to listen. And that may be exactly what you need now.

Let me give you a bit of relief: You don't have to be perfect. You don't have to pull yourself up by your bootstraps, kick up your heels, and keep on going. It's okay to stop and be honest about the failures and the mistakes and the pain. Sometimes life is simply really hard. Plans fail. Dreams go bust. Relationships fizzle. And our hopes are dashed. That's God's favorite time to hang out with us.

Jesus said, "Come to me, all of you who are weary and carry heavy burdens, and I will give you rest" (Matthew 11:28). He doesn't say, "Snap out of it!" No, He lays out a place for you to rest, waves His hand gently toward you, and says, "Come on, it's been a rough day; take a break and rest with Me."

And in that time of refreshment in His presence, we'll realize how God redeems our backstory so we can start over anew. That doesn't mean we won't occasionally still feel pain from our past—I know I still feel it from time to time. But God has begun a wonderful process of healing my wounds and giving me new legs to stand on. For the first time in my life, I'm ready to face down the villain on the battlefield.

Your Takeaway

Plot Points

- There's a story—a reason—behind everything we do.
- How we handle our backstory determines our future.
- Failure to get free from the weight of your past is one of the greatest limiting forces in your life.
- Healing begins through genuine self-awareness.
- Forgiveness requires your love; forgetting requires your strength.
- Once you've dealt with your forgiven past, learn to walk away from your guilt.

Dialogue with a Sage

- How have you handled dealing with people who have wronged you in your past?

- How has your backstory shaped who you are today?
- What are the most painful chapters in your backstory?
- What are the most important things you can do now to live free from guilt over the past?

From the Script

"Purify me from my sins, and I will be clean; wash me, and I will be whiter than snow" (Psalm 51:7).

chapter seventeen

STEPPING OUT

Movement, Risk, and Faith

The wind howled through the sails of their ships. Then louder, growing to a roar. The storm's gale force began to lift and toss the three wooden vessels as if seeking revenge upon them for venturing where they had no place.

On board each ship, the men's whitening faces were seared by pelting rain mixed with saltwater. The sailors were shouting, scrambling. Then stopping to hold on with white-knuckled claws. Each man silently wondered: *Is this it? The end? After all, no man should challenge God.*

The map they were following ended here. Beyond this point it showed no more land. No more mountains. No more coastlines and rivers. Only ocean. Deep, unforgiving, relentless ocean.

And perhaps more. At this edge of the map, a few words were written in simple longhand: *Monsters lie here.*

That's all they knew. And before now, it was enough to keep them away.

But men weren't made to follow maps; they were made to

prove them wrong. And that's exactly what Columbus and his crew did.

Why had they gone out? Why did they sail into the unknown? Why did any of the great explorers set forth and push doors open to undiscovered regions?

They went because their hearts burned within them. They explored because that's what they were made to do. They longed to be uncaged and uninhibited. They went to conquer fears, not be conquered by them.

The wildness of *what could be* pulled them away from the safety of life as they knew it. It called them away from normal and led them to their epic life, one without limits. Like Truman, they longed to know what lay beyond the horizon. And this longing led them to take risks and to keep moving forward.

A Closer Look at Greatness

This ability to keep moving forward is probably the key component of true greatness, the result of an unlimited life. But maybe you wince a little at that word *greatness*. For some reason, society and religion have taught us to interpret greatness as self-driven, godless ambition. We've believed that the pursuit of greatness is dark at its core.

That couldn't be further from the truth.

What is greatness? Is it superiority to others? Is it just standing out from the crowd? Are people who achieve greatness simply the ones who do more or better than everyone else? The ones who accumulate the most money, the most power, the most fame?

Hardly. Money will never define greatness; neither will power. And fame can never come close.

Probably the best word to describe greatness is *movement*.

To become great or unlimited literally means "to expand." The call to greatness isn't a challenge to be superior, but a challenge to be *more than you are right now*—that's the epic life. To keep moving forward and outward.

Paul understood this. He told us to "run in such a way that you will win" (1 Corinthians 9:24). And it's what he practiced himself—"I strain to reach the end of the race and receive the prize for which God, through Christ Jesus, is calling us up to heaven" (Philippians 3:14). True greatness is anchored in genuine humility and a belief that you can strive by God's strength to grow, expand, and influence beyond your current boundaries.

That's the epic life—to keep moving forward and outward.

Greatness begins with understanding the potential of a person fully surrendered to God. It means knowing that "with God everything is possible" (Matthew 19:26). The epic life fills the gap between what is and what could be, not only *with* God, but ultimately *for* God.

In generations past, the pursuit of greatness was not only admired but also encouraged. It was expected, not criticized. Young people were challenged to live epic lives. They were taught to make an impact and to live beyond themselves. Unfortunately, the same can't be said about most of today's generation. They've been largely robbed of the motivation to live great lives. I say it's time to take it back.

And the place to begin is to realize that the motion of greatness, this ever-expanding movement, has to begin with those few steps that break the inertia and get us going forward.

The First Step

It's true what they say: "The journey of a thousand miles begins with a single step." I know from personal experience.

In 1999, I was invited to be part of an expedition to the Annapurna Range in the Himalayas. I remember dipping down between the mountains in our small plane as we made our way from Kathmandu to Jomsom. My team told me the trek would take us over one hundred miles through winding valleys and treacherous mountains.

The more I'd heard about the intensity of the trip, the more tentative I became about it. I wasn't exactly in great shape, and I began to wonder if attempting the journey would be a mistake. By the time we strapped on our packs and prepared to launch out, I was downright doubtful. The guide gave me an out, telling me I could meet the rest of the team at the halfway point if I wanted. Of course that's not what I wanted. I wanted to start it and finish it.

"No, I'll be okay," I said. And with that, I simply lifted my boot and began the journey.

Was it tough? You bet it was. But the toughest part was that first step. It always is.

The hardest part of taking hold of your vision and living it out is simply breaking inertia and getting started. A lot of people have had great intentions of doing something and then never followed through to see it happen. Make sure you aren't one of them. Without that first step, dreams remain simply that, and goals fade into dimly remembered pictures of what life could have been.

Just Go

Jesus seemed to reinforce the idea of action wherever He went. In fact, *go* is one of the words we hear Him say time and time again. Often, after healing someone, He would say, "Go." When He finished preaching, He would tell the people to "go" and do what they just learned. When He was ascending into heaven, He commanded us to "go" and preach the gospel to every creature.

Jesus understood the importance of following words with action. He understood the power of picking up a foot once a decision has been made.

In the battle we face today, the villain very often wears the mask of Someday: Someday I'll begin working out. Someday I'll start reading. Someday I'll take the test. Someday I'll travel.

"Someday" is a big lie. The enemy's strategy is to keep us always focused somewhere off in the distance instead of on the challenge of moving off center today. Ecclesiastes says, "If you wait for perfect conditions, you will never get anything done" (11:4). It's true. If you wait until all your obstacles have been moved and the path is easy to travel, chances are, by then you may have lost your motivation.

> "Someday" is a big lie.

The time for action is now. The day for becoming the person God has clearly called you to be is today. This is your moment. This is your hour. You're the hero of your epic adventure, and all the characters in your story are watching. God is ready to charge with you against the forces of the villain, and He's patiently waiting for your signal.

But He won't force you. You see, one of the great mysteries of heaven is how God allows us to make our own decision about when and to what degree we allow Him to take the reins of our life. God has the armies of heaven assembled to back you up as you charge the hill of your greatest vision…but you have to be the one to give the war cry.

The Battlefield of Today

Welcome to the battlefield of today—where you're forced to make a daily decision about who you're serving. This is the place where the villain will use any means possible to trap you and trip you up.

He wants to get you moving as well—but moving in the totally wrong direction. Don't be fooled.

In fact, take a closer look at him. Sure, he looks confident. He's walking around shouting commands. With an air of authority he reminds you of your past mistakes.

But look past his guise. He tries to frustrate you, distract you, or scare you...but that's it. His tactics end there. You see, his hands are tied. His weapons are useless against a warrior or princess like you, someone sent and equipped by the King—for someone like that is far more armed and fortified than he is. Paul says, "We are human, but we don't wage war with human plans and methods. We use God's mighty weapons, not mere worldly weapons, to knock down the Devil's strongholds" (2 Corinthians 10:3–4).

That's why the enemy is so intent on distracting you from your goal. He'll do whatever he can to try and get your attention away from the heart of God. He'll try and deceive you into believing the lies of your false self and the lies of the world's attractions. He'll try to get you barreling down the fast road of filling your life with these empty diversions. Don't buy them. They're an illusion. All the stuff in the world will never compare to the satisfaction of fulfilling the thing for which you were born.

Master of Misdirection

Magicians drive me nuts. I'm the kind of guy who wants to know how things are done, and when I can't figure it out, it absolutely frustrates me.

A few months ago I was walking along the boardwalk in Fort Myers, Florida, and saw a crowd gathering. They were watching a magician perform. He did a few basic beachside stunts that you'd expect, then would every once in a while throw in an eyepopper. For the life of me, I couldn't figure out how he did some of them.

I've got a friend, a seeker, who owns a magic shop in Colorado Springs. Every once in a while, I'll stop by to say "hi" and he'll sucker me into buying a new gag. He's taught me that the key to illusion is the art of misdirection. Get the person watching to focus on the wrong thing and you can pull off almost any trick.

As we've said before, the villain is a master of misdirection. It's a wonder we still fall for his trickery, because it's so old. He used it against Adam when he misdirected his passion for God in the Garden. He used it against David when he misdirected his love for God with lust for Bathsheba. He tried to use it against Jesus when he attempted to misdirect His servanthood into selfishness. But Jesus didn't buy it. Not for a minute.

And you don't have to, either. It's the oldest trick in the book. Proverbs warns us, "Don't get sidetracked; keep your feet from following evil" (4:27). Don't go stepping down evil's pathway. That's misdirection, the mother of all illusions. You've got a better road to follow.

Misdirection is the enemy's way of getting back at God. The devil knows enough about the future to understand he doesn't have one at all, thanks to God. In his evil reaction, he knows that the most effective and destructive way to get back at God is to attack the object of God's affection—us. He does it by misdirecting the passion that's wired into us for God toward other things. Power, money, possessions, pleasure. Artificial romance in any form will work for the enemy if it keeps us from a genuine walk with God.

But God wants all of us. God told Moses, "Do not worship

any other god, for the LORD, whose name is Jealous, is a jealous God" (Exodus 34:14, NIV).

The villain realizes that when we encounter God and pursue Him, his battle against us is already lost, because God's jealousy protects anyone who's on His side. But if the enemy can get our affections and attention distracted and misdirected, he's certain that he's won.

Jesus said, "Ask and it will be given to you; seek and you will find; knock and the door will be opened to you. For everyone who asks receives; he who seeks finds; and to him who knocks, the door will be opened" (Matthew 7:7–8, NIV). What door? The door to life in God. A gateway that opens onto a lifelong road of following God in your epic story.

And it begins with your first step.

Needing a Nudge

I stood looking down from the top of the black diamond run at Copper Mountain. The wind had just kicked up and I clumsily zipped my jacket up to my eyes. *I'm a skier,* I thought. *What in the world am I doing strapped to a snowboard?*

Somehow, I'd let Clint convince me to give it a try. He told me it simply wasn't cool for a youth pastor to ski. I didn't really have an option. He'd gone for my weakness. He dared me, and that was all it took.

We made the first few runs on American Flier, a blue run in the middle of the park. By early afternoon I felt as though I'd been through Vietnam. My head was throbbing and my back and backside ached. I wasn't entirely sure my wrists were even still attached to my arms. I was cold and hot at the same time, and had snow jammed in places where snow just shouldn't be.

That's the problem with snowboarding. There's simply no

graceful way to fall. It's hard and fast. Anyone who's spent any time on a board knows what it's like to "catch an edge." That was the story of my first day.

Now, at the start of day two, I stood at the top of the hill and looked for Clint. He shouldn't have been too hard to find. Usually, he'd be jumping or flipping or grabbing his board in midair. But I couldn't find him. I'd lost the group somewhere between bailing off the lift and standing here, at the point of no return. To make things worse, I glanced over and saw the sign: Burn Run. I shivered at the thought of it. I pulled out my trusty map of the mountain and looked at a few of the other black runs. Widowmaker. Crusher. Devil's Fiddle, Dead Man's Run. It wasn't helping.

As I stood there, I began to rationalize why I didn't need to take the risk.

"It's probably not safe."

"What if I face plant and someone sees me?"

"I'll do it next time."

"It's time for lunch, anyway."

And then I found Clint. Actually, he found me. I never saw him, but I felt him. He gave me a friendly nudge from behind and I was off.

The next few minutes were thrilling, daring, and painful all at the same time. In the end, I survived Burn Run. And as I sat in the Lodge sipping hot chocolate, I did it as a different guy. I felt like a conquering hero returning to Rome. And all I needed was a little push.

Isn't it the same for you and me? We stand at the top of a decision looking down and contemplating our fate. We've had a few small successes, and we're feeling ready to go for it, but we're not sure how to start. For a lot of us the name of the decision could be enough to turn us away: Greatest Fear. New Relationship. Big Move. Different Job. We're anxious to experience the life God intends for us, but we've got to take the first step.

What would it take to move from where you are to where God wants you to be? Maybe it would just take a little push. I hope you're reading this book with someone you trust—a sage. Your sage is the perfect one to give you a little push in the right direction. But ultimately it's your own responsibility to make sure you aren't stuck.

If you've found yourself in a holding pattern in life, it's time for you to break out of it. DO SOMETHING. Stop thinking about someday and make it today.

> What will it take to move to where God wants you to be?

Abraham could have kept his tent stakes in the ground and never moved to the Promised Land. Gideon could have stayed in the safety of the winepress. Jesus could have stayed in the comfort of the carpentry shop. But that's not where greatness is lived out. The promise of an unlimited life means nothing if you don't answer it by picking up your foot.

Take the Risk

"It is only by risking that we live at all," William James said. It's true. Risk is a necessity in bursting limits. Consider any major limit-breaking event in history—the great discoveries, landmark legislation, even sports victories. Chances are, you'll find a significant series of risks taken.

Greatness takes risks. Greatness will risk reputation and relationship for the potential rewards, knowing that without risk, life is full of sameness. The same people. The same work. The same scenery. With it, life can be adventurous, daring, and different.

Risk isn't natural. It pushes against our instincts for safety and repetition. For sure, there's something in us that tends to lean toward the known rather than the unknown. But as T. S. Eliot observed, only someone who will risk going too far can possibly find out how far he can go. It wasn't until someone took the risk to do the impossible that we broke the four-minute barrier. It wasn't until someone took the risk to do the impossible that we landed a man on the moon. It wasn't until someone took the risk to do the impossible that the gospel spread across the world.

How far can you go for the glory of God? What risks will you take? What barriers will you break that you've avoided until now?

God Will Show You

God once spoke to Abraham and told him to pack everything up and move: "Leave your country, your people and your father's household." Funny thing was, God didn't tell him *where*. He simply said, "Go to the land I will show you" (Genesis 12:1, NIV).

Think of the weight of that. Abraham was seventy-five. He'd already built up his life and career. Now all that would change for…*who knows?*

I don't know about you, but I'd be nervous. But Abraham wasn't worried. His faith made the risk and the movement possible. "It was by faith that Abraham obeyed when God called him to leave home and go to another land…. He went without knowing where he was going" (Hebrews 11:8). Abraham had no idea what was at the end of the road, but he was willing to take it because he believed in the One who was calling him.

"Without risk, faith is impossible," Kierkegaard said. And we know that "without faith it is impossible to please God" (Hebrews 11:6, NIV).

Dangerous Prayers

There are some prayers that are safe. "God, please bless me." That's pretty tame.

But some prayers are dangerous. "God, I'll do whatever it takes to serve You." If you mean that, then you're in for it. "God, change me, work in me, shake me up." Now you've done it.

Those prayers are dangerous because they do something to ignite the process of change in you. A prayer like that gives God permission to prepare you for greatness. Prayers like that might even end up taking you through the wilderness, through what C. S. Lewis called a "spiritual trough or valley." If that happens to you, don't be discouraged; you'll come around sooner or later and experience the mountaintop.

It goes without saying that we've got to be careful in the decisions we make. But even worse is getting stuck in the mud of making no decision at all.

I'm often asked whether someone should take a particular risk or another. I've found that most times, the tougher decision is usually the best one. Remember the famous lines from Robert Frost?

Two roads diverged in a wood, and I—
I took the one less traveled by,
And that has made all the difference.

So don't be afraid to do something you've never done before. Go ahead, take the risk. Do the thing that's burning in your heart to do. Take the chance to dare greatly in your relationships, your health, your mind, and even in your walk with God. Pray the dangerous prayers your heart is dying to pray.

It will make all the difference.

Plot Points

- The key component of true greatness is ever-expanding movement and growth.
- The hardest part of accomplishing your vision is simply breaking inertia and taking the first step.
- The time for action is now.
- Stepping out usually requires risk and faith. Risk is a necessary element in living an unlimited life.

Dialogue with a Sage

- What are the greatest risks you've taken in life?
- Why is risk so necessary to a truly fulfilling life?
- What "dangerous prayers" are you praying?
- In what areas in life are you most likely to be stalled right now, blocked by inertia?
- For Life Unlimited, what action steps do you need to take *now?*

From the Script

Jesus said: "As the Father has sent me, so I send you" (John 20:21).

chapter eighteen

HANDLING CRITICISM

And Keeping the Dream Alive

I should have braced myself, but I wasn't prepared.

In 2000, when I first began to tell people I felt like God was moving me from youth ministry to start something new, I got hit.

I absolutely knew that what I was about to do was the right thing. I knew I'd been on the mountaintop and heard from God. I was sure that, like Moses, it was written plainly on my face. Apparently it wasn't. And I wasn't ready for the response.

What made the criticism I encountered especially difficult was the fact that it came from some of the people I love and respect the most. I remember telling a few of my friends about my vision, only to be met with blank stares and raised eyebrows. I remember feeling totally deflated, wondering if I'd heard God at all. One of my friends actually said my new idea wasn't from God at all, but a distraction from the enemy. One day I'd been walking on air; now I was dragging on the ground.

Dousing the Flame

If we allow it, criticism can be one of the most destructive tools of the enemy to discourage the call of God in our lives.

Like me, you've felt it, too. Maybe you had an idea for a new ministry or a new business or some new direction in life. You really believed it was the right way for you, and inside you'd been thinking about it and processing it and even praying about it. The candle's flame began to grow. And then someone douses it with a bucket of cold water.

The result probably left you feeling empty and even a bit foolish. For a lot of us, that's when we give up.

David is a great example of holding on in spite of unfair criticism. He'd been sent out from the family farm to deliver food to his brothers fighting on the front lines against the Philistines. He got there just in time to see the enemy giant, Goliath, step forth and taunt the army of God's people, making them retreat in fear.

But David wasn't like them. He saw a different picture. He saw God being insulted, and there was no reason to let it continue. "Who is this uncircumcised Philistine that he should defy the armies of the living God?" (1 Samuel 17:26, NIV). Then David went around voicing his God-given perspective to the soldiers.

When Eliab, David's oldest brother, heard him speaking with the men, he burned with anger at him and asked, "Why have you come down here? And with whom did you leave those few sheep in the desert? I know how conceited you are and how wicked your heart is; you came down only to watch the battle." (1 Samuel 17:28, NIV)

In one fell swoop David was accused of irresponsibility, arrogance, and insignificance.

It happens all the time, especially with people we're closest to. Often the ones who love us the most are also the ones who hurt us the most with

> Often those who love us most also hurt us most with their words.

their words—our friends, our parents, and even our pastors. It's because they're the ones we're most influenced by.

I remember how easily I was influenced when my older sisters thought something I was doing was stupid. Because of their opinions, I've broken up with girls, changed my college major, and regularly switched fashion. If we let it happen, other people's opinions and criticism can be a powerful limiting force.

Ugly Baby?

A dream is our baby.

Have you ever seen an ugly baby? Sarah and I are relatively new parents and one of the weird things about having a baby is wondering if your infant is attractive or not. Of course all babies are wonderful, but some are simply cuter than others.

One of my favorite *Seinfeld* episodes was about the "man baby." A friend of Jerry's had an infant who looked like it had the face of an old man. The baby was excruciatingly ugly. In the episode, Jerry and George didn't know quite know how to respond to the parents. And of course when Kramer saw the baby, he couldn't keep from gasping and jerking and bracing himself against the wall. It was funny on the show, but it's not funny at all when it happens to our dreams in real life.

"Your dream is ugly," the villain begins to whisper. "That'll never work." If you allow it, that voice of the villain will keep you boxed in.

What if David had listened to the voice of the villain through his brother? What if he'd allowed the enemy to convince him to tuck his tail and run home to the sheep?

The villain loves to speak his lies to us through the words of others. The villain even whispered his lies to Jesus through Peter, so that Jesus had to turn to Peter and tell him, "Get away from me, Satan! You are a dangerous trap to me. You are seeing things merely from a human point of view, and not from God's" (Matthew 16:23). People who criticize our dreams may also be seeing things only from a human point of view instead of God's viewpoint. But their remarks can still hurt.

I remember telling one friend in particular about my new idea. He responded by telling me all the reasons it wouldn't work. I smiled and listened and acted as though I were unaffected by his words. But I bit my lip as I left the meeting that night. I got into my car, drove for a few minutes, then turned into a parking lot near an empty field. I remember walking up a hill in the darkness, staring at the solitary light on the top of Pikes Peak. It felt as though another chapter of my painful backstory was forming. Only this time, I was the one pulling the rug out from under myself.

Maybe he's right, I actually thought. *Maybe I never really heard from God in the first place.* I wondered how I could have believed so intensely in something so foolish.

But as I stood there in the cool night air...I began to weep. Not for the words my friend had so carelessly pierced my heart with. I wept for an idea that had nearly died. I wondered how someone could hold on to an idea as dearly as I was holding on to mine. It's not as though it were a person I was holding onto. Or was it?

The Bible tells us this about Jesus: "Everything got started in him and finds its purpose in him" (Colossians 1:16, *The Message*). When our lives are surrendered to the Lord, ideas that are born in the heart of God can then be carefully transplanted into ours. These ideas and visions that He instills within us are God's way of advancing His purposes on Planet Earth. Each of us is responsible for doing our part in fulfilling that purpose.

So hold fast to your idea, your vision. You may soon be taking the hill on the battlefield of tomorrow. Don't let anyone's criticism today stop you from preparing and moving forward to the battle.

Critics Have Their Place

Please don't get me wrong. Critics do have their place. And not all criticism is poison. After all, even critics are sometimes right.

And there's a fine art in deciphering truth from venom. It can mean the difference between a renegade dream and a well-laid plan to accomplish God's vision. Ignoring something that can make you better is as much a crime as crushing another's dream.

The Bible says, "Wounds from a friend can be trusted" (Proverbs 27:6, NIV). If a friend, especially a sage, is warning you or exposing a weakness in your armor, don't be stubborn. Allow God to work through them. Always stay humble and teachable, while at the same time holding on to the things God has burned into your heart. Take time to process what's said to you. Take what applies and throw out what doesn't. Getting defensive won't help you in the long run.

> Not all criticism is poison.

Even in my loneliest moment on the hill that night, I knew there was some truth in the words I'd heard. My friend had advised me to start slow and focus my vision. It felt like a wet blanket at the time, and I ignored it and passed it off as the villain's message. But it wasn't the villain's message, and in the end I could have avoided some pitfalls in the pursuit of God's plans for me.

Stealing from Yourself

So it's absolutely vital to learn to discern between the voice of a sage and the voice of discouragement—especially when the voice is your own. One of the worst critics of all is the one who looks most like us.

God plants a dream in our heart, He architects a future for us—then we ourselves discredit it by bemoaning the way He made us. I'm not sure there's any greater insult to God than to deny who He created us to be. After all, a life surrendered to Him is not ours, but His. And we ought to allow Him to accomplish whatever He wants in us and through us, in whatever way He wants.

I used to have a bad habit of telling others what I wasn't good at: "Oh, I'm not really the pastor type. I'm just not good at it. I don't really care much for people." I'd criticize myself. I began to realize that criticizing myself was actually nothing more than self-pity and pride. Who am I to tell God that He didn't do a good job with me? Who am I to tell Him that in my case He probably should have taken a bit more time? That's ridiculous and dangerous.

The Bible says, "Destruction is certain for those who argue with their Creator. Does a clay pot ever argue with its maker? Does the clay dispute with the one who shapes it, saying, 'Stop, you are doing it wrong!' Does the pot exclaim, 'How clumsy can you be!'" (Isaiah 45:9). So be careful not to argue with God. When we turn inward and begin to tear away at the person God has made us, we're stealing from our-selves the treasure of God's calling that He placed within us.

If you've found yourself criticizing your own actions and thoughts and abilities…stop it. Take your eyes off yourself and put them back on God where they belong. After all, He's the one who gave you your dream to begin with.

What are the dreams God has given you? What's the baby you've introduced to the world? Have you thrown it away simply because someone else didn't like the shape of its nose or the color of its hair or the sound of its voice?

Winning Glory for God

David didn't let the criticism of his brothers get him down. He stayed focused, and eventually found himself face-to-face with Goliath. By holding on to the vision God had given him, he gave God the opportunity to refine and deepen that vision with staggering foresight. David boldly proclaimed in the giant's hearing:

> "This day the LORD will hand you over to me, and I'll strike you down and cut off your head. Today I will give the carcasses of the Philistine army to the birds of the air and the beasts of the earth, and the whole world will know that there is a God in Israel. All those gathered here will know that it is not by sword or spear that the LORD saves; for the battle is the LORD's, and he will give all of you into our hands."
> (1 Samuel 17:46–47, NIV)

That boldness won him Goliath's head, and ultimately the crown. Even more important, it won glory for God, just as David said it would. And the same thing will happen as you hold on to and live out the vision God has given you, no matter what others say about it.

Your Takeaway

Plot Points

- If we let it, criticism from others can be one of the enemy's most destructive tools in discouraging us from following God's call in our lives.
- Often the ones who have the most power to discourage us in following God's call are those whom we love most.
- Criticism can also be valuable if we respond to it and evaluate it properly.
- When we criticize or think poorly of ourselves, we are actually criticizing God.

Dialogue with a Sage

- When has the criticism of others caused you great discouragement in doing what you believed God wanted you to do?
- When others criticize your plans or dreams or goals, how can you go about determining whether there is value in their criticism, or whether you should ignore it?
- How can criticism from others help to strengthen your commitment to your God-given purpose and calling?

From the Script

"Mark out a straight path for your feet; then stick to the path and stay safe. Don't get sidetracked; keep your feet from following evil" (Proverbs 4:26–27).

part five

THE
RESOLUTION

chapter nineteen

FOCUS AND REFOCUS

For a Sure and Certain Victory

One of the biggest differences between people who have the privilege of living out their magnificent obsession and those that are merely hopeful is simply the power of focus.

One way to become more effective in every area of the 252 Matrix is to stop dabbling. In each area, *focus!* Learn to discipline yourself to do a few things exceptionally well. Be sure to give each area attention, but don't try to do too much in one particular area.

I've learned that lesson the hard way too many times. In high school, I tried to earn my pilot's license at the same time I was trying to work toward ordination in ministry, and I ended up with neither. In the early nineties, I tried to run a business while pastoring a large youth group, and my lack of focus on the store ultimately cost me the business.

A few years ago, I had two very strong ideas for books, but I was unable to give either the proper focus; they're both half completed in my computer.

"No one can serve two masters," Jesus said (Matthew

6:24). They say if you chase two rabbits at once, you'll get neither. Paul talked about focusing all his energies "on this one thing" (Philippians 3:13). David's heart cry was for "one thing"—the presence of God (Psalm 27:4). Learn to be focused, and you'll find yourself more effective and less frustrated. Look one-eyed at your vision and then run after it with everything you've got.

Refocus on Your Calling

So you've determined to live fully engaged in every area of life and you've decided never again to accept average. You've faced down the pain of the past, and you're determined to trust God with your life by focusing on His call and ignoring the enemy's misdirection that tries to attach itself to your heart.

As you're doing these things, you still know you aren't perfect, but chances are, they're beginning to work. You've broken inertia and begun to see small successes. Your confidence is beginning to strengthen. And then come bigger successes...and even bigger.

That's the time to beware. We can get distracted by achievement. There's something about "making it"—in relationships, in business, or even in ministry that has a way of drawing our eyes off God and onto ourselves. If we start to get consumed by the lure of success, it becomes very difficult to think straight.

A few weeks ago, I was driving in the mountains of Colorado on the way to a cabin where I like to do a lot of my writing. It was dark outside, and snow had begun to fall in big flakes. At first it was pretty awesome watching the snow as it danced in front of my headlights. Then it began to fall harder. Soon I felt like I was in a scene from *Star Trek* as I sat mesmerized by the snow swirling at me in a hypnotic pattern. It took everything I had to focus on the road and not the snow.

Sometimes success is just like that. Its lure of success is so powerful, it has a way of getting our eyes off the One who gave us the dream to begin with. We look to ourselves and look away from the God who is greatness Himself. And that's when the trouble starts.

So with every achievement, with every goal you attain, take time to stop and go back to your original calling. If you find yourself off track or off-kilter, take time for a personal retreat and get refocused and recalibrated with the heartbeat of God. Don't fool yourself into thinking everything is okay. Success without God is no success at all. Saul experienced that tragedy; so did Solomon. But you never have to.

> Success has a way of getting our eyes off the One who gave us the dream.

If you've found yourself distant from Him, do whatever it takes to rekindle your first love. If you've found yourself distracted by success, make the tough decision to drop it and get away with God. That's what David did, both when he sinned and when he succeeded—he always went to God.

The Measure of Success—Giving It Away

In the end, the measure of your success is not awards you receive or the money you amass. God reminds us, "Those who love money will never have enough. How absurd to think that wealth brings true happiness!" (Ecclesiastes 5:10). The measure of our success isn't in what you've achieved in this preamble to eternity. Rightly, the measure of your success is in how much you're giving away.

To reach your life's end and to have loved God with all

your heart, all your soul, all your strength, and all your mind—to be empty at the end of it all, and yet still have a heart that longs to give more—that is to have lived a Life Unlimited.

And if you've spent all your heart and soul and mind and strength that way, and in the unique way that only *you* could—then you'll for sure have left a matchless legacy for all who come behind you.

Press On

"We are God's household," the Bible says, "if we keep up our courage and remain confident in our hope in Christ" (Hebrews 3:6).

So my final charge to you is this: Remain confident. Hold on to everything God has planted deep in your heart. You're a valiant warrior. You're a hero. Therefore, "be strong and steady, always enthusiastic about the Lord's work, for you know that nothing you do for the Lord is ever useless" (1 Corinthians 15:58). Always remember that as long as you're living fully engaged for God, your life is never lacking in meaning.

When I began this book nine months ago, I was focused on writing it for you, because I'm absolutely confident in this message. And with that in mind, I told a good friend that I fully intended to write my life's great work, my magnum opus. He smiled, as if he knew what was going to happen. And in the end, I've written much of this book for myself. I can tell you that the process of etching my thoughts onto the page have in turn etched them even deeper into my heart.

My prayer is that they've also motivated you, challenged you, and encouraged you. Whether or not this is my magnum opus is yet to be determined. If I'm fortunate enough to live to God's limit, I have another eighty-seven years to answer that.

Meanwhile, I hope you'll continue to join me in pulling every bit of life out of every blessed day that God gives us.

Press on, hero. I'll see you on the journey. Carpe diem!

Your Takeaway

Plot Points

- Discipline yourself to do a few things exceptionally well.
- Achievements can distract you from God and from your life's mission. That's why it's important to take time and get refocused on your calling from God.
- Success in life is measured not by your achievements or wealth, but by how much of yourself you have given away.

Dialogue with a Sage

- After the experience of going through this book, restate your life's purpose and calling from God as you now understand it.
- Review also the life-list of personal goals you prepared in chapter 3. What refinements would you now make in that list? What are the most important items on this list for you to take action on right now?

From the Script

"Make the Kingdom of God your primary concern" (Matthew 6:33).

FROM STRENGTH TO STRENGTH

s we pulled up to the house on a beach near Charleston, Sarah and the kids and I were rushed by a mob of cousins and uncles and aunts. It felt so good to see them.

Sarah's parents had rented this house on the beach and invited us to come and join them for a week. So for the next several days we swam in the ocean, played in the pool, built sand castles on the beach, and grilled out almost every night. We created memories to last a lifetime. But the greatest memory was a simple walk on the beach.

It connected two points of my pilgrimage.

The sun was setting, and the usual Atlantic breeze had calmed as Sarah and I kicked off our sandals and headed down the beach. Our two boys straggled behind us, carrying buckets and picking up broken pieces of shells that would become a treasured collection.

We breathed deeply, taking in the smell of salt and sea. From off in the distance somewhere, we heard someone playing an old Jimmy Buffet song.

My mind drifted back and forth across the ten years since the beginning of my journey—since our walk together on the beach in Fort Myers, Florida. I felt as though I'd lived a lifetime since then. I had faced my greatest fears and wrestled with my life's purpose. I'd been stretched and challenged in every area of my life. And to top it off, my deepest wounds had been reopened and my heart had been exposed.

I felt a bit like a soldier fresh off the front line. But I also truly felt alive. I had, as Psalm 84 says, set my heart on pilgrimage (v. 5, NIV). The prayers I'd whispered ten years earlier were being answered. My desire to experience life fully and richly and deeply was being satisfied. I had stepped out of the comfort of the sidelines and onto the front line. I'd chosen my side, and an epic had begun. I'd taken the place as the hero of my story, and I'd determined to live beyond the limits of average.

I couldn't say my life had become easier, but I knew I'd become stronger. Actually, I had *discovered* my strength.

Let's go back and take another look at Psalm 84.

> *Blessed are those whose strength is in you,*
> *who have set their hearts on pilgrimage.*
> *As they pass through the Valley of Baca,*
> *they make it a place of springs;*
> *the autumn rains also cover it with pools.*
> *They go from strength to strength,*
> *till each appears before God in Zion.*
> *Hear my prayer, O LORD God Almighty;*
> *listen to me, O God of Jacob. (vv. 5–8, NIV)*

The Valley of Baca mentioned here may be a figurative name, since the word *Baca* is like the Hebrew word for "weeping." The psalmist may be telling us there'll be times of struggle and tears through which we must pass on our pilgrim journey. But in such struggle, we can find all the strength we need in God—and from this experience of strength comes blessing.

I've discovered what it means to really lean on God; there was nothing else for me to depend on. And in my doing that, God has taken me "from strength to strength."

The psalmist goes on to say,

> Better is one day in your courts
> than a thousand elsewhere;
> I would rather be a doorkeeper in the house of my God
> than dwell in the tents of the wicked.
> For the LORD God is a sun and shield;
> the LORD bestows favor and honor;
> no good thing does he withhold
> from those whose walk is blameless. (vv. 10–11, NIV)

One day with God. Better than all the fame or money or achievement in the world. That's the point of life. Nothing can replace the life and power and fulfillment of God's presence.

And what's the result? Is there a prize for the hero? A treasure? No doubt the presence of God is reward enough. But God goes even further: "No good thing does he withhold from those whose walk is blameless." *Blameless.* That's you and me after the cross. And to us is promised *every* good thing—

- friendships that last a lifetime…
- total health with energy till your last breath…
- joy in the everyday moments of life…
- ideas right from the throne room of heaven…
- and undying passion for God to drive it all.

Now that's living!

O Lord Almighty,
blessed is the man who trusts in you. (Psalm 84:12, NIV)

When it all comes to a close, the person who wins is the one who trusts not in himself but in God. In ourselves we can do little, but with God nothing is impossible.

So go for it! Determine to live the life God so desperately wants you to live. Your epic life is waiting for you. Today, make the decision never to accept average again. Choose your side. Take hold of the life God has for you—grasp and never let go of your Life Unlimited.

My story continues from here. Yours is up to you.

Hero, this is not the end. It is just…

THE BEGINNING

Once upon a time…

ACKNOWLEDGMENTS

I have discovered that writing is not a solo effort. I would like to thank Sarah, my wife and best friend, for enduring the many days of thinking and reading and writing with me.

Thanks to Thomas Womack, my editor and writing sage, for your patience and tireless effort. Thank you for not accepting average; you're a craftsman in the first degree.

Thanks to Doug Gabbert, Don Jacobson, and all my friends at Multnomah; you've caught a vision for an unlimited generation.

Thanks to Christopher Beard, for your enduring friendship through everything.

Thanks to Layne Schranz, Jim Stack, Susan Blaha, and Tamra Farah, for your helpful eyes on the manuscript.

Robert Blaha and Barry Farah, you are so much more than board members or sages; you are true friends.

Ted Haggard, my pastor and friend, thank you for giving me the backdrop for this book and the freedom to discover unlimited living.

Thanks to Terry and Linda Felber for letting me escape to your beautiful home as I developed this project.

Thanks to the many who have encouraged me, guided me, and never allowed me to accept average: my dad, Rod Bolin; Peter and Susan Roehl; Frank and Terry Serpe; Butch and Tammy Maltby; Bruce Nygren and Brandon Beatty, Doug Littlejohn, Cliff Taulbert, Michael Broome, and Dick Schultz.

Thanks to my dear siblings: Brigit Elliott, Susie Collins, Sally Butler, Mary Hrbek, and Luke Bolin; you've carried on the legacy well.

And finally, a special thanks to Starbucks Coffee and Sarah Waters for the white chocolate mochas and daily encouragement. I love and thank you all.

The publisher and author would love to hear your comments about this book. *Please contact us at:*
www.multnomah.net/johnbolin